AMERICAN RIGHTS

FREEDOM OF ASSEMBLY

STEPHEN F. ROHDE

☑®
Facts On File, Inc.

Dedicated to my wife Wendy, my children Dana, Evan, and Tessa,
and my granddaughter Lexie.

May they all live in a country that remains faithful to the Bill of Rights.

Freedom of Assembly

Facts On File, Inc.
132 West 31st Street
New York NY 10001

Library of Congress Cataloging-in-Publication Data
Rohde, Stephen F.
Freedom of assembly / Stephen F. Rohde.
    p. cm.—(American rights)
Includes bibliographical references and index.
ISBN 0-8160-5663-3 (alk. paper)
1. Assembly, Right of—United States—History. I. Title. II. Series.
KF4778.R64 2005
342.7308'54—dc22   2005000684

Facts On File books are available at special discounts when purchased in
bulk quantities for businesses, associations, institutions, or sales promotions.
Please call our Special Sales Department in New York at (212) 967-8800
or (800) 322-8755.

You can find Facts On File on the World Wide Web at http://www.factsonfile.com

Text design by Erika K. Arroyo
Cover design by Pehrsson Design
Maps and graphs by Dale Williams

Printed in the United States of America

VB FOF 10 9 8 7 6 5 4 3 2 1

This book is printed on acid-free paper.

Contents

Acknowledgments

⚜

During the year I spent on this book, my colleagues in our law practice, Greg Victoroff and Michele Friend, carried an extra share of responsibility, freeing me to do my research and writing, for which I am genuinely grateful.

Gwendolyn Crawford and Celeste Chretien deserve special thanks for the skills, support, and patience they devoted to helping me write this book.

Much of this book, particularly the periods covering my own lifetime, reflects my deep respect for hundreds of people of conscience whom I have known who have marched, rallied, demonstrated, and protested in support of what they believed in. This book is infused with the spirit of all those who have exercised their freedom of assembly, freedom of association, and the right to petition for redress of grievances.

The history of these fundamental rights may be written by scholars, but it is lived by courageous people who have the audacity to take the Bill of Rights seriously.

Introduction

Freedom of assembly, freedom of association, and the right to petition the government for redress of grievances are often overshadowed by other rights enshrined in the First Amendment to the U.S. Constitution, such as freedom of speech, freedom of the press, and freedom of religion. Yet the rights of assembly, association, and petition have served equally vital roles in the development of American democracy, political dissent, and individual autonomy.

Freedom of assembly encompasses a wide array of activities including holding a meeting, organizing a protest march, staging a rally, convening a conference, going on strike, picketing a business, or doing any number of things in which a group of people come together for a common, lawful purpose. Freedom of assembly is expressly guaranteed in the First Amendment to the U.S. Constitution.

Freedom of association is the right of people to be together and to form and join organizations that serve a common, lawful purpose. Freedom of association is not mentioned in the First Amendment but has been developed through decisions of the U.S. Supreme Court.

Freedom to petition the government for redress of grievance means the right to bring problems and concerns to the attention of elected and appointed officials at all levels of government in an effort to have them "redressed," or corrected. The right to petition is expressly guaranteed in the First Amendment.

NATION OF JOINERS

Alexis de Tocqueville, a French writer who visited the United States in 1831 and later wrote *Democracy in America,* said America would become a nation of joiners and club-formers. It has become that and a lot more through the tumultuous exercise of these fundamental rights. The struggle to win the right to join with other like-minded people links more than 800 years of history, from the Magna Carta in 1215 through the Revolutionary War and the anti-slavery, women's labor, civil rights, and antiwar movements down to the present day and the emergence of the Internet. Unlike other constitutional rights, freedom of assembly and freedom of association are *collective* rights, which cannot be exercised or enjoyed by a single individual but depend instead on groups of individuals joining together for a common purpose.

These rights can be traced to the oldest instincts of human beings to form tribes and to cooperate for their mutual protection and survival. People need and benefit from interaction in groups. This explains the popularity of the expression "there is strength in numbers."

In ways often overlooked, American independence was prompted by the failure of King George III and the British Parliament to address the long stream of petitions begging for the redress of grievances. The American colonies organized opposition to the Stamp Act and Townshend Acts through nonimportation associations, committees of correspondence, petitions, assemblies, congresses, and the famous Boston Tea Party. The vibrancy of courageous revolutionaries meeting together, often in secret, gives life to the story of American independence.

The First Continental Congress in 1774 brought together extraordinary men such as John Adams, George Washington, and Patrick Henry. The very first use of the term *Bill of Rights* comes in 1774 in the "Declaration and Resolves of the American Continental Congress containing the Bill of Rights, a list of grievances," including "a right peaceably to assemble, consider their grievances, and petition the King."

And the Declaration of Independence, drafted by Thomas Jefferson but informed by hundreds of petitions throughout the colonies, contains at the very top of the list of grievances against King George III the disruption of colonial legislatures, the embodiment of the right to assemble.

The creation of the U.S. Constitution by 55 delegates assembled in Philadelphia in summer 1787 was itself a historic exercise of freedom of assembly by the founders. The Bill of Rights, written by James Madison at the First Congress in 1789 in New York City, guaranteed, among a handful of preeminent liberties, "the right of the people peaceably to assemble, and to petition the Government for a redress of grievances." Madison had a rich history to draw upon, including the constitutions of the individual states, many of which anticipated the Bill of Rights by protecting these fundamental freedoms.

FREEDOM FOR MANY COMMUNITIES

Freedom of assembly, freedom of association, and the right to petition the government for redress of grievances each played a vital role over the span of American history, in every key movement that has shaped the nation, beginning with the abolition of slavery.

Embedded in the Constitution itself and left intact in the Bill of Rights, slavery persisted in American life; only a civil war would end it. But before and after that bloody war, antislavery societies and abolitionist groups aggressively exercised their freedom of assembly to demand the elimination of slavery. Despite the passage of the Thirteenth, Fourteenth, and Fifteenth Amendments to the U.S. Constitution, efforts to maintain segregation were opposed by the collective efforts of people in the North and South to bring about true freedom, again by means of organizations and persistent pleas to the government. The emergence of the National Association for the Advancement of Colored People (NAACP) and its continuous battles in the courts to ensure the right of association is central to this story.

Freedom of assembly played a vital role in the momentous growth in the Civil Rights movement. From *Brown v. Board of Education* in 1954 to the courageous story of Rosa Parks, from the demonstrations in Greensboro, North Carolina, to the Freedom Riders, from the Congress of Racial Equality (CORE), to the "Freedom Schools," and the March on Washington in August 1963 led by the Reverend Martin Luther King, Jr., culminating in the Civil Rights Act of 1964 and the Voting Rights Act of 1965, the right to assemble and protest have been indispensable.

Left out of the Constitution and the Bill of Rights, women would have to mount their own movement to seek equality, and to do so they would turn to their freedom of assembly, association, and petition. Powerful women such as Elizabeth Cady Stanton and Lucretia Mott convened a historic conference for women's rights in Seneca Falls, New York, in 1848. Margaret Sanger gathered people together to fight for birth control. Susan B. Anthony organized the Woman's Suffrage Convention and Parade in 1915 and the campaign for the Nineteenth Amendment, led by the National Woman Suffrage Association and the National Woman's Party.

Steadily throwing off the burden of stereotypes and discrimination, women emerged in every field of endeavor to participate in public life, including various organizations across the political spectrum. However, true equality remained elusive, prompting the campaign for the Equal Rights Amendment (ERA) and culminating in the 1976 ERA Parade, which nonetheless failed to win the support of a sufficient number of state legislatures to ratify the amendment.

For generations in America, working men and women did not enjoy the right to assemble together in unions to bargain for safe working conditions and fair pay. The emergence of the labor movement was all about the freedom to assemble and the freedom to associate, including labor picketing, marches, and strikes.

In all of this, the Supreme Court has been asked to interpret the scope and limitations imposed on these fundamental rights. The clashes between police and angry demonstrators protesting wars, abortion, globalization, civil rights, and virtually every public policy issue confronting America, including pivotal events such as the Nazis' march in Skokie, Illinois; antiwar protests; and the internment of Japanese Americans during World War II, have prompted key court decisions attempting to strike a balance between liberty and order. In every era governments have sought to limit these freedoms and suppress dissent. American history has been marred by periods when officials have tried to mute the voices of protest.

FREEDOM ON THE INTERNET

As the 21st century begins, Americans wonder how the Internet will affect freedom of assembly and association and the right to petition. As new generations of Americans grow up in a world dominated by interactive Internet communications (and older generations strive to catch up), it remains to be seen whether mass demonstrations, protest rallies, and marches will give way to cyber-assembles. New causes and organizations may find it easier (or harder) to attract members and advance their agenda in the new Information Age. Perhaps the Internet will revolutionize the use of online petitions to influence government policy and reform the country's problems. Perhaps this new technology will cause a highly diverse nation to splinter into isolated interest groups; or perhaps it will serve to link the country as never before through a nationwide online town meeting. These and other provocative issues will frame an examination of the future of freedom of assembly, freedom of association, and the right to petition the government for redress of grievances.

Historical Origins of Freedom of Assembly

Freedom of assembly and the right to petition can be traced back more than 800 years to England. A clash between a king and his subjects prompted one of the most important chapters in the history of personal freedom.

THE MAGNA CARTA

In 1215, a civil war was raging in England. The wealthy and powerful barons had lost confidence in King John after he lost a war with France. Taxes on the barons to pay war debts were overwhelming. King John ruled like a tyrant. In January 1215, a group of barons demanded a charter of liberties to protect them against the king's unjust rule. In May 1215, the barons took up arms against the king and captured London. To put an end to the conflict, the king and barons agreed to a peace treaty. In 63 paragraphs, the Great Charter, or in Latin, the *Magna Carta,* signed on June 10, 1215, at Runnymede, England, by the river Thames, would change the world.

The Magna Carta was revolutionary. For the first time in history, a king had guaranteed certain rights to his subjects and put it in writing. Beyond guaranteeing those rights, the Magna Carta created a means to enforce them. It stated that if ever the king deprived anyone of their "lands, castles, liberties or rights," the king would restore them at once. And if any disagreement arose, "let it be settled by the judgement of twenty-five barons."

> "The greatest constitutional document of all times—the foundation of the freedom of the individual against the arbitrary authority of the despot."
>
> —*English judge Lord Denning, in 1956*

The Grand Council

Twenty-five barons, who would become known as the Grand Council, would assemble to decide disagreements between a king and his subjects. This was freedom of assembly. This had never happened before. For centuries, as long as anyone could remember, kings and queens had ruled with absolute power—indeed, by "divine right." They claimed that their absolute power derived from God and could never be questioned.

There were no elections. There were no legislatures to debate and write laws. The law was totally under the control of the monarchy. The Magna Carta changed all that. The Grand Council represented the first time in Western history that an assembly of individuals was established with authority *over* the king.

The Community of the Whole

The Magna Carta stated that if the king or any of his servants "offend in any way . . . then those twenty-five barons together with the community of the whole land shall distrain and distress us in every way they can, namely seizing castles, lands and possessions . . . until in their judgement amends have been made."

The phrase "the community of the whole land" is one of the earliest references to what would later become known as "the people." This is important because it acknowledges the existence of "the people" as a "community," an entity with a collective identity separate from each individual.

Freedom of assembly and freedom of association are based on the notion that there is something special and distinct in a group or community separate and apart from the individuals that make up that group or community. As early as 1215, in the Magna Carta, this "community" is not only recognized, it is respected by the king, the most powerful person in the realm.

By its terms the Magna Carta protected only the rights of wealthy barons. Yet it set a precedent in England and later in America. For almost 800 years, the Magna Carta has stood as a symbol of placing limits on power and protecting the rights of those who are subject to that power. In every time and place where leaders have tried to exercise unrestrained authority, trampling on personal liberties, the Magna Carta has been cited in opposition. Nowhere did the Magna Carta have greater meaning than in

America where a new nation rebelled against another English tyrant.

THE DECLARATION OF INDEPENDENCE

The Declaration of Independence, signed on July 4, 1776, announced to the world why the American colonies were throwing off the bonds of tyranny and forming a new nation. The Declaration reflects the importance of both the freedom to assemble and the right to petition the government for redress of grievances. The men who conceived of declaring independence from England came together to debate and deliberate on the reasons that caused them to forge a new nation. What no single person could do, many were able to achieve by assembling. And what they produced—the Declaration of Independence—was itself a petition addressed to King George III and to the entire world, declaring the causes and conditions justifying their revolution.

Origins of the Declaration

Grounded in its own time and place, the Declaration was hardly written in a vacuum, disconnected from the illuminating history so familiar to the men who wrote it. The Declaration is part of a long stream of important historical documents stretching back hundreds of years, first in England and later in America, that addressed the most fundamental questions facing society.

Colonial Assemblies

By 1765, the American colonies were struggling under oppressive laws passed by the British Parliament and abusive practices imposed by King George III. Every time the colonies resisted, the king punished them more severely. Time and again the colonies sent petitions to the king and to Parliament pleading with them to reverse their course and to stop the economic and political oppression of the colonies. Loyal to the Crown, the colonists hoped that these petitions would convince the king to respect the American colonies and to attend to the problems they were suffering.

The colonial assemblies proved to be a hotbed of resistance to England. The very name "assemblies" demonstrated the importance

THE MAYFLOWER COMPACT

In 1620, even before they had set foot on the New England coast, the Pilgrims met together aboard their ship, *The Mayflower,* to agree upon the form of self-government under which they would conduct themselves in their new home. They wrote the Mayflower Compact, which would become an honored part of American history, with its solemn undertaking to "covenant and combine ourselves together into a civilly body politick, for our better ordering and preservation and furtherance of the ends aforesaid." Here are the seeds of the American identity and consciousness: A free and independent people, facing an uncertain future, having the courage and strength to "combine ourselves" for the purpose of governing their society, to "enact, constitute, and frame, from time to time, as shall be thought most meete and convenient for the general good of the Colonies, unto which we promise all due submission and obedience."

Inhabiting a new land, these new Americans were forced to depend on themselves for their sustenance, their survival, and their progress. They had to make daily decisions for themselves without depending on a distant monarch, whether benevolent or despotic. Americans would have to make their own way—*together.*

they placed in the right of assembly. Gathered together, the members of these assemblies were able to exchange ideas about the growing desire for independence from England and debate the risks and opportunities posed by such a bold move.

No issue proved more irritating to the colonies than the taxes imposed on them by King George III. In 1765, the assembly in Charleston, South Carolina, announced that "it is inseparably essential to the freedom of a people and the undoubted rights of Englishmen that no taxes be imposed upon them but by their own consent." This would become the resounding demand: "No taxation, without representation!"

Later that same year, the Massachusetts assembly, known as the Great and General Court of Massachusetts, called for a congress of all colonies to meet in New York to consider *unified* action. Thirteen separate assemblies were one thing, but a single, united congress was something far more powerful. Again, its strength would arise from the force of *collective* action taken by individuals gathered together in one place.

The congress opened in October 1765 in New York City. Delegates arrived from throughout the colonies. One remarked that it was "an Assembly of the Greatest Ability I ever saw."

Not only were the delegates openly declaring their "natural and inherent rights," they were openly exercising them, including the right to freely assemble. Soon they accomplished their first act of unified effort, a Declaration of Rights and Grievances, a powerful petition that called on the king to stop his violations.

By February 1768, the Massachusetts Legislature had denounced the Townshend Acts as "taxation without representation" and sent their pronouncements to the rest of the colonial assemblies, with a call for united action.

The impact of what Massachusetts had done can be measured by the uproar it caused in England. Lord Hillsborough accused the Massachusetts legislators of conspiring to "promote unwarrantable combinations, and to excite an unjustifiable opposition to the Constitutional authority of Parliament." The royal governors of the other colonies were instructed to order their assemblies to ignore Massachusetts or else be dissolved, which is exactly what happened to the Massachusetts Assembly. It was dissolved until it mended its ways due to its "rash and hasty proceedings."

It is particularly noteworthy that Lord Hillsborough was so upset by Massachusetts's effort to "promote unwarrantable combinations." Hillsborough knew full well that the assemblies and the congress were a serious threat to the king. He realized that to maintain order he might have to go so far as to disband these gatherings since, if left unrestrained, they served as a breeding ground for revolutionary ideas and plans.

When the colonies would not relent, assembly after assembly was dissolved. Indeed, England's use of the unchecked power to dissolve the assemblies themselves—to literally deny freedom of assembly to the colonists—became a new outrage for those most committed to the cause of independence.

> "[We must] stand on the broad and common ground of natural and inherent rights . . . as men and descendants of Englishmen! . . . There ought to be no New England men, no New Yorkers . . . but all of us Americans!"
>
> —*Christopher Gadsden of South Carolina, 1765*

Denied their assemblies, the colonists proved resourceful in finding other ways to gather their strength. In the Carolinas, self-appointed legal bodies were formed, calling themselves "regulators." By 1772, pockets of resistance were organized, calling themselves "Sons of Liberty." In Massachusetts, Samuel Adams, a leader in the fight against British colonial rule, revived the earlier Committees of Correspondence, which established a network of members exchanging news and information, first in Boston, then throughout Massachusetts and soon in all the colonies. In time, riders on horseback were traversing the countryside carrying letters and pamphlets containing expressions of hope and protest, reassuring far-flung communities that they were not alone.

In spring 1774, the Virginia Assembly, known as the House of Burgesses, declared, "A Congress should be appointed . . . from all the Colonies to concert a general and uniform plan for the defense and preservation of our common rights." The response was overwhelming, and all the colonies except Georgia sent delegates to Philadelphia in September 1774 to convene the First Continental Congress. The first to speak, John Sullivan of New Hampshire, announced that his instructions were less than revolutionary: "to devise, consult, and adopt measures to secure and perpetuate their rights, and to restore that peace, harmony and mutual confidence which once subsisted between the parent country and her colonies."

Meanwhile, back in Massachusetts, a different group had met in Suffolk County and issued the Suffolk Resolves, declaring that the people of that state should form a government of its own, collect taxes, and withhold them from England until the abusive acts that had been unilaterally imposed were repealed. When word of the Suffolk Resolves reached the Continental Congress, pandemonium broke out, and the resolves were promptly approved and adopted.

The congress proceeded to declare no less than 13 acts of Parliament to be illegal. This alone was unprecedented. A group of self-appointed renegades had convened themselves into a legislative body, without any permission from the Crown, and had presumed to declare more than a dozen Acts of Parliament to be illegal and therefore not to be obeyed. To implement the decisions of the congress, a Continental Association was formed. As of December 1, 1774, all imports from England were to cease. A committee was to

COMMON SENSE

As the War of Independence raged, leaders spread the word defending their rebellion and seeking wider support. In January 1776, Thomas Paine, an English journalist who had arrived in America little more than a year earlier, wrote a highly influential pamphlet titled *Common Sense,* in which he attacked the British monarchy and treated Americans as a distinct people, who deserved to rule themselves. *Common Sense* was phenomenally successful, selling 120,000 copies in barely three months and galvanizing popular support for the war against England.

be elected in every city, town, and county to enforce the decrees of the association.

As the delegates prepared to leave, they realized that the work of the congress belonged to no single delegate. Congress had acted as a unified body speaking with one voice. By exercising their freedom of assembly, the delegates had experienced the power of collective action. The exercise of the freedom of assembly was in full bloom. They were courageous, believing themselves endowed with certain natural rights, and did not wait for the permission of any ruler to come together with a common purpose. The ability of the colonies to overcome regional differences and forge compromises fostered a strong sense of unity and common purpose.

On April 18, 1775, war broke out. British troops encircled the Massachusetts towns of Lexington and Concord. By the next day, the British had sustained 273 casualties; the Americans, 95. The American Revolution had begun.

In April 1776, the Second Continental Congress opened direct trade with every nation in the world except Great Britain and a month later advised the colonies to establish their own state governments. These were bold steps taken by the revolutionaries to emphasize their unwavering commitment to independence.

Free and Independent States

On June 7, 1776, Richard Henry Lee, delegate from Virginia, offered a bold motion: "That these United Colonies are, and of right ought to be free and independent States, that they are absolved from all allegiance to the British Crown, and that all political connection between them and the State of Great Britain is, and ought to be totally dissolved." Congress postponed a final vote until July, to allow a committee to write a formal declaration of independence.

This painting by Jean-Léon Gérôme (1863–1930) depicts Thomas Jefferson, Benjamin Franklin, and John Adams reviewing a draft of the Declaration of Independence. *(Library of Congress, Prints and Photographs Division, LC-USZC4-9904)*

On June 12, 1776, five men were appointed to the drafting committee: Thomas Jefferson, John Adams, Benjamin Franklin, Roger Sherman, and Robert R. Livingston. This so-called Committee of Five delegated the writing of the first draft to Jefferson. In a matter of a few days, Jefferson prepared his draft, Adams and Franklin made some editorial changes, and they submitted their history-making work to the Congress.

The Declaration of Independence was not written to express the abstract ideas of a small group of political theorists. In fact it was the outgrowth of a collaborative effort of people inside and outside the Second Continental Congress reflecting ideas and complaints long held throughout the colonies. Almost 100 petitions, resolutions, and instructions were issued between April and July 1776 by various states, counties, towns, grand juries, and private and quasi-public groups, enumerating the serious injuries visited upon the American colonies and calling for independence from Britain. Yet again, here was the impact of people assembling in towns and villages throughout the colonies, taking time from family and work to exchange ideas, to debate the most important issues of the day, and to reflect their collective will in written documents expressing their demand for justice and self-government.

The Preamble served to announce to the world that the inhabitants of America considered themselves "one people," who were entitled to the rights enjoyed by their fellow British subjects. This was as much a Declaration of Equality as a Declaration of Independence.

The Preamble certainly did not mince words. Previewing the detailed accusations to follow, the Preamble charged in strong and uncompromising terms that the king's history of injury and injustice amounted to tyranny. Elsewhere, the Preamble declared that in such cases it is the people's "right, it is their duty, to throw off such Government, and to provide new Guards for their future security."

A Bill of Particulars

Despite the enduring popularity of the Preamble, to the men who wrote and signed the Declaration of Independence, the list of 28 grievances against King George III was the heart of the document. Here, the Declaration reads like a criminal indictment cataloguing a long series of accusations against the British monarchy and the

> "We hold these truths to be self-evident, that all men are created equal, that they are endowed by their Creator with certain unalienable Rights that among these are Life, Liberty, and the pursuit of Happiness."
>
> —*Preamble to the Declaration of Independence, 1776*

Parliament. And at the very top of the list of grievances are a group of charges condemning the king for disrupting the colonial legislatures, calling them together and then dissolving them at whim, refusing to assent to laws duly passed and failing to enforce those he had approved.

The preeminence given to these charges reflects the high value the founders placed on freedom of assembly. For the colonists, no right was more important than the right to assemble in duly constituted legislatures to debate and enact the laws under which they and their families would live and work. It was the height of tyranny for the king to disrupt and ignore these assemblies and the laws they passed.

At the center of the list of grievances is the key accusation that the king had joined with the British Parliament to impose upon the colonies taxation without representation, striking at the fundamental proposition that government must be based on the consent of the governed. It was one thing for colonial legislatures acting through duly elected representatives to levy a tax for the common good but it was an outrage for the British Parliament, where the colonies had no representation, to do so.

The final accusation against King George III and the concluding paragraph of the Declaration constitute the formal declaration of independence. The document reminds the world that at every stage the Americans had sought redress, but they were met with "repeated injury." Furthermore, the colonists had appealed to their fellow "Brittish brethren" for justice, only to be ignored.

The Declaration was the last resort when repeated petitions seeking the redress of grievances were ignored. The colonists, as British subjects, had taken seriously their right to petition their government to correct and improve their condition. Their loyalty had been freely given in exchange for a fair and just ruler, not one who ignored their grievances. But King George III had misjudged his subjects, presuming their loyalty was unconditional, requiring nothing from him in return.

The Declaration of Independence ends with a "mutual" pledge; an announcement to the world that these men, assembled together in summer 1776, were united in the common cause of independence. Many battles lay ahead. Many would not see the day of true independence. This was only a *declaration* of independence. The actual creation of a new nation would await victory on the battle-field and then in future assemblies where the very right to assemble and petition the government for redress of grievances would be enshrined in a Bill of Rights.

THE U.S. CONSTITUTION

In summer 1787, 55 delegates to the Constitutional Convention met in Philadelphia. Eleven years earlier America had first declared and then won its independence. To organize their new nation the founders had assembled and written the Articles of Confederation, which served as the *first* constitution of the United States. But the articles, which established a loose alliance of 13 fiercely independent states without any national government, proved unwieldy and inefficient.

Consequently, George Washington, Alexander Hamilton, James Madison, and others, fearing that America would never reach its promised greatness, called for a gathering of delegates from all the states to amend the Articles of Confederation.

The Constitutional Convention

What the delegates did in Philadelphia in 1787 was far more than amend the Articles of Confederation. They quickly tossed aside the articles and drafted a brand-new charter for America: the United States Constitution. Through debate and compromise, some honorable, some expedient, some shameful, the delegates hammered out a new plan of government with three branches: legislative, executive, and judicial.

The Constitutional Convention represents yet another historic example of freedom of assembly in action. Delegates from diverse backgrounds, occupations, experiences, and political viewpoints assembled to design a plan of self-government. The result was the establishment of a national government. Most of the rules and procedures for running that government were in place and have continued to this day, subject to relatively few amendments.

Where Is the Bill of Rights?

With the Constitution drafted, some delegates felt something was missing. As he joined two of the remaining 39 delegates in refusing

This illustration depicts Benjamin Franklin speaking at the Constitutional Convention in Philadelphia in 1787. *(Library of Congress, Prints and Photographs Division, LC-USZ6-1737)*

to sign the new Constitution, Virginia delegate George Mason put it: "I would sooner chop off this right hand than put it to a Constitution without a Bill of Rights."

In the final days of the convention, eager to finish their hard work, the delegates had rejected Mason's call for a bill of rights. He reminded them that most of the states had adopted a bill of rights, or Declaration of Rights, guaranteeing personal liberties and that the new national Constitution should do no less. When Mason's pleas were rejected, the majority of delegates set the stage for a battle that almost prevented the new Constitution from taking effect.

The adoption of the Constitution in September 1787 did not make it into law immediately. It still had to be ratified by the states. Ratification debates would last for the next two years, centering primarily on the glaring absence of a bill of rights.

This debate was nowhere more intense than in Virginia, where George Washington and James Madison fought for ratification, and George Mason and Revolutionary War patriot Patrick Henry fought against it. Madison conceived of a brilliant strategy. He urged Virginians to ratify the Constitution and to elect him to the First Congress, where he would personally propose a Bill of Rights.

Madison's idea worked. Virginia joined the necessary number of states to ratify the Constitution, and it became the governing charter of the United States of America.

Writing a Bill of Rights

On April 1, 1789, the House of Representatives met in New York City for the first time in history. This was the First Congress, and everyone arrived with a sense of urgency and purpose: The laws of the new nation were to be written.

No one arrived with a more energetic agenda than James Madison. Madison had been a prominent leader at the Constitutional Convention in Philadelphia two years earlier. Madison wanted to make the Constitution "as acceptable to the whole people of the United States as it has been . . . to a majority of them." The amendments would prove that the supporters of the Constitution "were as sincerely devoted to liberty and a republican government" as any of its opponents.

Eight states had submitted proposed amendments. There was broad consensus that the Constitution should specifically protect certain rights, including the "right of petition and assembly."

On June 8, 1789, during a lengthy speech, Madison listed the rights he thought were most justified, and among them was the right to "peaceable assembly." Madison urged that the "people shall not be restrained from peaceably assembling and consulting for their common good; nor from applying to the Legislature by petitions, or remonstrances, for redress of their grievances." While the first draft of what would become the First Amendment contained no mention of freedom of assembly or the right of petition, a select committee on July 28, 1789, added the right to assemble and redress grievances.

On August 24, the House approved and sent to the Senate 17 amendments, but the Senate did not get around to debating them until September 2. By September 10, the Senate had refined the list to 12 amendments, including the right to peaceably assemble and petition.

Representatives of the House and Senate then met to reconcile the different versions of the amendments. Certain rights were combined. Freedom of assembly and the right to petition the government for redress of grievances were formally included in what would become the First Amendment.

On September 24, by a vote of 37 to 14, the House approved 12 amendments, and the next day the Senate followed suit. The amendments, described as the Bill of Rights, were sent to the states for ratification by President George Washington on October 2.

During the ensuing debate over the ratification of the Bill of Rights, some of the amendments generated strong and conflicting views, but by all accounts freedom of assembly and petition did not. These were seen as fundamental rights that deserved protection under the Constitution.

On December 15, 1791, after two years of debate and discussion, Virginia became the final necessary state to ratify the last 10 of the 12 proposed amendments, officially adding the Bill of Rights to the Constitution.

In considering the addition of a Bill of Rights to the U.S. Constitution, Congress was not writing on a clean slate. The individual state constitutions contained declarations of rights. Many of them expressly protected freedom of assembly and the right to petition the government for redress of grievances (see Appendix).

The ratification of the Bill of Rights was a historic moment. For the first time a national constitution containing a written guarantee of certain fundamental rights had been approved. Among those rights were the freedom to peaceably assemble and the right to petition the government for redress of grievances.

This portrait of James Madison, who wrote the Bill of Rights and served as the fourth president of the United States, was painted by Gilbert Stuart (1755–1828). *(Library of Congress, Prints and Photographs Division, LC-USZ62-13004)*

The Bill of Rights is a set of solemn promises. It guarantees that the government will respect the most cherished rights of the people. Given the breadth and detail of the Bill of Rights, no country had ever done this before.

But making a promise and keeping it are two different things. It was one thing for the Bill of Rights to be written, approved, and ratified. Only time and history would tell whether the government would remain faithful to the Bill of Rights.

2

Slavery and Suffrage

Dr. Martin Luther King, Jr., said that the arc of history bends toward freedom. The history of the struggle for civil rights in America demonstrates that the arc did not bend on its own. It was forced in the direction of freedom through outspoken leadership and millions of courageous individuals who risked life and limb to organize, in small groups and eventually in vast numbers, first to abolish slavery, then to eliminate segregation, and eventually to enact civil rights laws prohibiting discrimination and requiring equal treatment.

The struggle for civil rights for people of color and equal rights for women in America is a testament to the vital role of freedom of assembly, freedom of association, and the right to petition the government for redress of grievances. Every chapter in that story reveals how time and again progress was made only when people organized groups, boycotts, marches, and demonstrations. These assemblies strengthened the movement by reassuring activists that they were not alone and by forcing the rest of the public to acknowledge the justness of their demands.

THE INSTITUTION OF SLAVERY AND ITS ABOLITION

In 1790, 14 years after the Declaration of Independence boldly announced that "All men are created equal" and two years after the ratification of the U.S. Constitution, which was intended to "establish justice" and "secure the Blessings of Liberty," there were 500,000 slaves in America. The Constitution failed to abolish slav-

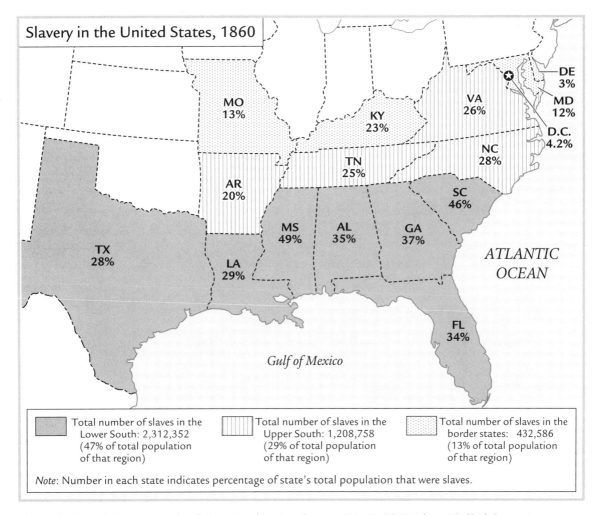

Slavery in the United States, 1860

DE 3%
MO 13%
KY 23%
VA 26%
MD 12%
D.C. 4.2%
TN 25%
NC 28%
AR 20%
SC 46%
TX 28%
MS 49%
AL 35%
GA 37%
LA 29%
ATLANTIC OCEAN
FL 34%
Gulf of Mexico

Total number of slaves in the Lower South: 2,312,352 (47% of total population of that region)

Total number of slaves in the Upper South: 1,208,758 (29% of total population of that region)

Total number of slaves in the border states: 432,586 (13% of total population of that region)

Note: Number in each state indicates percentage of state's total population that were slaves.

The institution of slavery was deeply ingrained in American society. In 1860, almost half of the entire population of the Lower South was composed of slaves.

ery and instead perpetuated it, and by 1860 there were 4 million slaves in America.

Slavery was tightly woven into the fabric of society, from its economy and laws to its social structure and culture. So powerful was the institution of slavery that even prestigious men such as Thomas Jefferson and George Mason (who owned slaves) and Benjamin Franklin and John Adams (who did not) could not bring it to an end. Indeed, it took a bloody civil war to accomplish that and yet another century for most of the stains of slavery to be cleansed, even as the residue of racism remains to this day.

Abolitionist meetings were being organized throughout the North, generally in the big cities such as Boston, Philadelphia, and New York. In this period there was an outpouring of support from abolitionists to free the slaves. In the early 1860s, Congress was deluged with emancipation petitions. Exercising, in its purist form, the right to petition the government for redress of grievances, opponents of slavery implored Congress to act.

On January 1, 1863, President Abraham Lincoln issued the Emancipation Proclamation, which declared slaves free in those southern states fighting against the Union in the Civil War, but he ignored the slaves in the Union itself. Since the proclamation failed to abolish slavery throughout the country, it prompted even greater antislavery activity.

Slaves stand in front of a building on Smith's Plantation, Beaufort, South Carolina, circa 1862. *(Library of Congress, Prints and Photographs Division, LC-USZ62-67819)*

FREDERICK DOUGLASS

In 1838, 21-year-old Frederick Douglass, a slave in Baltimore, escaped to the North from bondage. Having somehow learned to read and write, he became the most famous black man of his time. Through his writings and lecturing he became a leader of the abolitionist movement.

Douglass's skill as a public speaker moved his audiences to question the country's dependence on slavery. On the Fourth of July, 1852, he gave an Independence Day address in which he asked, "What to the American slave is your Fourth of July? I answer, a day that reveals to him more than all other days of the year, the gross injustice and cruelty which he is the constant victim."

In 1843, Douglass participated in the Hundred Conventions project, a six-month tour of meeting halls throughout the West organized by the American Anti-Slavery Society to bring the cruel reality of slavery to wider public attention. Despite the fact that Douglass and those who came to hear him were exercising their constitutional rights, some of the events were disrupted by pro-slavery mobs. In Pendleton, Indiana, Douglass's hand was broken by a gang of thugs. In 1854, he spoke at a conference of blacks and declared that the antislavery movement "is emphatically our battle; no one else can fight it for us."

By summer 1864, abolitionists had gathered an unprecedented 400,000 signatures urging Congress to pass legislation to abolish slavery. This was the greatest collective use of the right to petition since the enactment of the First Amendment 75 years earlier. The Senate had already adopted the Thirteenth Amendment abolishing slavery, and with this show of public support the House of Representatives followed suit in January 1865.

It is often overlooked that the liberation from bondage of hundreds of thousands of slaves constituted the largest *strike* in American history. Former slaves walked off the job, bringing many plantations to a halt and preventing the South from maintaining its army. By April 1865, General Robert E. Lee, in charge of the rebel forces, had surrendered to General Ulysses S. Grant, leader of the Union forces.

RECONSTRUCTION

In the wake of the Civil War, blacks in many parts of the South began to exercise their newly won freedom, forming their own churches and organizing politically, Blacks began to be elected to state legislatures in the South. After 1869, two blacks, Hiram Revels and Blanche Bruce, were elected to the U.S. Senate, along with 20 black congressmen. These numbers would drop sharply after 1876, with only one black left in Congress by 1901.

"REMEMBER THE LADIES"

The struggle to abolish slavery coincided with the movement of women to secure equal rights, most importantly the right to vote. The history books are filled with the story of the Boston Tea Party, when on December 16, 1773, 50 colonists protested oppressive British import taxes by boarding three English ships while masquerading as Mohawk Indians and throwing chests filled with tea into the sea. But little is written about the Boston Coffee Party, organized in 1777 by the Daughters of Liberty, to protest the exorbitant price of coffee. It was one of the first actions taken by revolutionary women, who also formed groups to support the cause of independence, boycott British goods, make their own clothes, and purchase only goods made in America.

Despite the fact that Abigail Adams, wife of John Adams, a delegate to the Constitution Convention and second president of the United States, urged her husband in a letter to "remember the ladies," the rights of women would be largely ignored by the "founding *fathers,*" leaving women to their own devices in the struggle to gain equal rights. Even Thomas Jefferson, who wrote in the Preamble to the Declaration of Independence that "All men are created equal," offered the patronizing observation that women in America would be "too wise to wrinkle their foreheads with politics."

The independence won in the Revolutionary War hardly made women independent. When the 13 colonies wrote new state constitutions, only New Jersey guaranteed women the right to vote, and that provision was repealed in 1807. New York, where the Bill of Rights was drafted in 1789, made it clear that only men enjoyed the right to vote by granting it specifically to "mates."

It would take another 130 years of organizing, marching, and protesting for women to secure the right to vote. Only by gathering in ever-larger groups and organizations were women (and their male allies) able to build a national movement that demanded the attention of those in power, all of whom were men. By exercising their freedom of assembly, freedom of association, and their right to petition the government for redress of grievance, women expanded their role in a democratic society and moved closer to equality with their male counterparts.

The challenge was daunting. For centuries women had been excluded from political life and confined to the home, the church, and the school.

Even when female reformers such as Harriet Martineau mustered the courage to question such suffocating conventions in her book *Society in America,* one reviewer cautioned that women should not read the book: "Such reading will unsettle them for their true stations and pursuits and they will throw the world back again into confusion."

"[I]n whatever situation of life a woman is placed from her cradle to her grave, a spirit of obedience and submission, pliability of temper, and humility of mind, are required from her."

—The Young Lady's Book of 1830

Working for Equality

If women's rights were equated with a state of "confusion," how would they ever achieve the equality promised by the Declaration of Independence? The answer first began to emerge in the workplace. As the American economy grew, so did the demand for labor. Workers were needed to make an ever-expanding array of goods and products, which drew women away from their homes and into factories and workshops. Women were not allowed to become lawyers, doctors, or professors, so they were relegated to low-paying, menial jobs. Women earned 25 to 50 percent of what men made for the same job. In the fast-growing textile industry, most of them were between 15 and 30 years old. According to Eleanor Flexner in *A Century of Struggle,* by 1836 a woman's daily average wages were less than 37½ cents, and thousands earned as little as 25 cents a day, working as long as 12 to 16 hours a day. Consequently, some women were making less than two cents an hour. Women knew they were being exploited and began to do something about it, not as individuals but through collective action—they went on strike.

Faced with intolerable circumstances, the first known strike of women factory workers took place in Pawtucket, Rhode Island, in

> "The first object of laudable ambition is to obtain a character as a human being, regardless of the distinction of sex."
>
> —A Vindication of the Rights of Women, *the first defense of equal rights for women, written by an English schoolteacher, Mary Wollstonecraft, 1792*

1824, when 202 women refused to work in protest over a wage cut and longer hours. The next year, the United Tailoresses of New York went on strike, demanding higher wages. Four years later in Dover, New Hampshire, women went on strike, parading with banners and flags.

In 1834, in Lowell, Massachusetts, a group of young women went on strike after a coworker was fired. A newspaper account reported that one of the women climbed on top of the town pump and made "a flaming Mary Wollstonecraft speech on the rights of women and the iniquities of the 'money aristocracy . . .'"

The women's strikes became more militant and urgent. One resident of Chicopee, Massachusetts, reported that on May 2, 1843, there was a "[g]reat turn out among the girls . . . after breakfast this morning" in a "procession preceded by a painted window curtain for a banner" that began with 16 marchers and grew to 44.

This brief glimpse reveals the essential power of individuals coming together for a common purpose. At first, a few began a strike, then many joined them, using any means at their disposal ("a painted window curtain for a banner"). Women in small towns would risk public ridicule for having the audacity to challenge their employers and condemnation for making "a spectacle of themselves."

Organizing for Equality

Reaching the next level of organization, also at Lowell, Massachusetts, a group of women in 1844 formed the Female Labor Reform Association, which published a series of pamphlets titled "Factory Tract." In one vehement passage, they described the women in the textile mill as "nothing more or less than slaves in every sense of the word! Slaves, to a system of labor which requires them to toil from five until seven o'clock, with one hour only to attend to the wants of nature, slaves to the will and requirements of the 'powers that be' . . ."

Meanwhile, in New York City in the 1840s, women workers were also actively organizing. In 1845, the New York *Sun* newspaper published a notice titled "Mass Meeting of Young Women," calling on "young women of the city engaged in industrious pursuits" to attend "a mass meeting in the Park" for a rally and speeches.

In tandem with their efforts in factories and textile mills, women were also making steady progress in the field of education. In 1821, Emma Willard founded the Troy Female Seminary, the first recognized institution for the education of girls. In 1843, Harriet Hunt, who had twice been refused admission to Harvard Medical School, organized the Ladies Physiological Society. And in 1849, Elizabeth Blackwell established the New York Dispensary for Poor Women and Children.

COMBINATIONS

In 1845, the New York *Herald* reported that about "700 females" had met "in their endeavor to remedy the wrongs and oppressions under which they labor," but separately editorialized that ". . . we very much doubt whether it will terminate in much good to female labor of any description. . . . All combinations end in nothing."

To many women, there was a double standard at work here. "Combinations" of capital at textile mills or large city newspapers were accepted as a useful and necessary part of a growing and expanding economy, but "combinations" of employees seeking to improve their working conditions were dismissed by some as useless, futile, and even harmful. In the women's movement, as in other minority movements throughout American history, those who had not yet achieved equal rights had to rely on their right of assembly and association to overcome resistance from those who already enjoyed equality.

Proponents of the women's movement argued that those in power took for granted their own right to assemble and associate among themselves. They felt that well-established individuals saw this as the natural consequence of their position in society as the leaders of industry, the professions, government, and the courts. When it came to the efforts of women to alter the existing power structure in order to gain equality, they found it indispensable to organize, meet, and multiply the impact of what any one of them could accomplish alone. In responding to the New York *Herald's* claim that "combinations end in nothing," women in the movement were urging that "combinations end in change."

Early efforts by women to organize and protest were directed at the social problems caused by alcohol. *(Library of Congress, Prints and Photographs Division, LC-USZ62-111068)*

Women were also beginning to make inroads by gaining admission to college. At Oberlin College in Ohio, Lucy Stone, active in a peace society and in the antislavery cause, organized a debating club for girls. After she was chosen to write the commencement address, she was told it would be read by a man. She refused to write it.

Viewing their own subjugation as a form of slavery, the emerging women's movement was deeply sympathetic to the cause of abolishing slavery. Women joined antislavery societies and devoted untold hours to gathering signatures on petitions to Congress. Seeing their struggle for equality inextricably linked to the abolitionist movement, women took time away from their own struggle for equality in order to petition the government to end slavery.

Still, women met together to discuss their own struggles. In a key event that combined the impact of freedom of assembly, freedom of association, and petitioning the government, women from all over the country met in Seneca Falls, New York, to discuss the future of women's rights.

Seneca Falls Convention

In 1848, Elizabeth Cady Stanton and Lucretia Mott convened the first Women's Rights Convention in Seneca Falls, New York. Stanton, who had tried in 1840 to attend the World Anti-Slavery Society Convention in London, where women were not admitted, concluded that the only way to confront the oppression of women "was a public meeting for protest and discussion." For two days in July, 260 women and 40 men came together to share their experiences and organize the future of their movement. In the end, 68 women and 32 men signed a Declaration of Sentiments and Resolution, echoing the Declaration of Independence, whose promises of equality for "all" had proven so hollow to anyone except white males.

After the Civil War, Stanton, an advocate for both the abolition of slavery and equal rights for women; Susan B. Anthony, an outspoken Quaker who traveled widely organizing support for women's right to vote; and Sojourner Truth, an escaped slave who devoted her life to writing, preaching, and lecturing against slavery and in favor of equal rights for women, tried to include women in the new constitutional amendments guaranteeing rights to former slaves. The Fourteenth Amendment defined citizens as "all persons born or naturalized in the United States" and guaranteed equal protection of the laws—but in referring to the electorate, it introduced the word *male* into the Constitution for the first time. The Fifteenth Amendment declared that "the rights of citizens . . . to vote shall not be denied or abridged . . . on account of race, color, or previous condition of servitude." Women of all races were still excluded.

It was intolerable to Anthony that women could not vote. In 1872, she went to the polls in Rochester, New York, and cast a

> "Today, countless file boxes in the National Archives in Washington bear witness to that anonymous and heart-breaking labor. The petitions are yellowed and frail, glued together, page on page, covered with ink blots, signed with scratchy pens, with an occasional erasure by one who fearfully thought better of so bold an act. . . . They bear the names of women's anti-slavery societies from New England to Ohio."
>
> —*Eleanor Flexner,*
> A Century of Struggle, *1959*

ballot in the presidential election, an act that was against the law. She was arrested, convicted, and fined $100, which she refused to pay. In 1875, the Supreme Court in *Minor v. Happersett* held that while women may be citizens, all citizens were not necessarily voters, and states were not constitutionally required to allow women to vote.

Victory for Women's Suffrage

At the dawn of the 19th century, Carrie Chapman Catt and the National American Woman Suffrage Association organized a huge lobbying effort of millions at every level of government. Alice Paul and the National Woman's Party, a smaller group, not only lobbied but conducted direct action, including marches,

Women seeking the right to vote became highly visible during suffrage parades (1913). *(Library of Congress, Prints and Photographs Division, LC-B201-3643-12)*

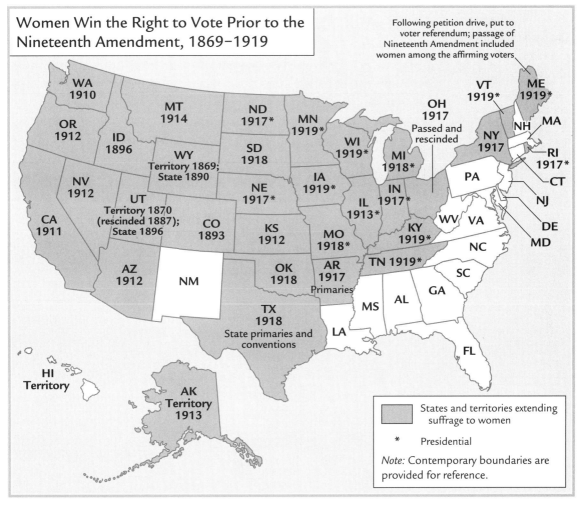

Women Win the Right to Vote Prior to the Nineteenth Amendment, 1869–1919

Following petition drive, put to voter referendum; passage of Nineteenth Amendment included women among the affirming voters

WA 1910
OR 1912
ID 1896
MT 1914
ND 1917*
MN 1919*
WI 1919*
MI 1918*
OH 1917 Passed and rescinded
VT 1919*
ME 1919*
NH
MA
NY 1917
RI 1917*
CT
NJ
DE
MD

NV 1912
UT Territory 1870 (rescinded 1887); State 1896
WY Territory 1869; State 1890
SD 1918
IA 1919*
IN 1917*
PA
CA 1911
CO 1893
NE 1917*
IL 1913*
KY 1919*
WV
VA

AZ 1912
NM
KS 1912
MO 1918*
AR 1917 Primaries
TN 1919*
NC
SC
GA

TX 1918 State primaries and conventions
OK 1918
LA
MS
AL
FL

HI Territory

AK Territory 1913

Legend:
Grey shading = States and territories extending suffrage to women
* Presidential
Note: Contemporary boundaries are provided for reference.

Women secured the right to vote in state elections before they were guaranteed the right to vote in federal elections. By the time the Nineteenth Amendment was ratified in 1920, women were already voting in state elections in 16 states.

boycotts, picketing at the White House, and civil disobedience. A powerful movement in support of a woman's right to vote was emerging.

The Nineteenth Amendment affirming that very right swept through Congress in 1919. After getting more than half the state ratifications needed in the first year, the amendment ran into opposition from states' rights advocates, the liquor lobby, business interests opposed to higher wages for women, and even some

"The right of citizens of the United States to vote shall not be denied or abridged by the United States or by any state on account of sex."

—*The Nineteenth Amendment to the U.S. Constitution, 1920*

women themselves, who accepted claims that the amendment would threaten the American family.

Finally the ratification process narrowed down to a six-week battle in Tennessee. The fate of the Nineteenth Amendment was literally decided by a single vote. Harry Burn, a 24-year-old legislator, switched from "no" to "yes" in response to a letter from his mother saying, "Hurrah, and vote for suffrage!"

Women had achieved the right to vote and blacks had achieved freedom from slavery, but much remained ahead of them to ensure an equal place in American society. Looking back, women and people of color could thank freedom of assembly, freedom of association, and the right to petition for redress of grievances for helping them overcome the oppression they had suffered. Without these critical rights—and without courageous people to exercise them—the history of America would hardly be the same.

3

The Labor Movement

The dawn of the 19th century brought an expansion of industrialization into the cities as well as the mechanization of farms, prompting a demand for millions of low-paid workers to ensure a continuous supply of goods and services to the growing American population. The owners' goals were productivity and profit, which meant long hours with little pay for workers.

THE RISE OF LABOR UNIONS

In Philadelphia in 1829, at one of the first city wide gatherings of labor unions, a speaker asked whether the American Revolution had been fought "to crush down the sons and daughters of your country's industry under . . . neglect, poverty, vice, starvation, and disease." While businesses were free to incorporate (between 1790 and 1860, 2,300 new corporations were chartered), when workers attempted to form trade unions, the courts ruled that they were illegal "conspiracies" in restraint of trade. In New York, for example, 25 members of the Union Society of Journeymen Tailors were found guilty of "conspiracy to injure trade, riot, assault, battery." The judge ruled: "In this favored land of law and liberty, the road to advancement is open to all. . . . Every American knows that or ought to know that he has no better friend than the laws and that he needs no artificial combination for his protection. They are of foreign origin and I am led to believe mainly upheld by foreigners."

To protest the ruling, 27,000 people gathered at City Hall Park and formed a Committee of Correspondence, which defiantly organized a convention of mechanics, farmers, and working men

> "We find ourselves oppressed on every hand—we labor in producing all the comforts of life for the enjoyment of others, while we ourselves obtain but a scanty portion, and even that in the present state of society depends on the will of employers."
>
> —*Anonymous, 1827*

in Utica, New York. The convention drafted its own Declaration of Independence and established an Equal Rights Party. Thus, a setback in court that threatened to eliminate any legal protection for unions prompted an ambitious response, which itself depended on freedom of assembly and association.

Soon the Equal Rights Party was holding rallies across the country. In Philadelphia, 20,000 people gathered in Independence Square. In New York, a meeting was called: "Bread, Meat, Rent and Fuel! Their prices must come down. . . . All friends of humanity determined to resist monopolists and extortioners are invited to attend."

In this environment, by 1835, 50 different trades had organized unions in Philadelphia, calling a general strike demanding a 10-hour work day. Soon Pennsylvania and several other states had enacted such laws, reinforcing the workers' belief that strikes could be effective in helping them gain better working conditions.

In 1835, there were 140 strikes in the eastern part of the United States. In one, 1,500 men, women, and children went on strike for six weeks.

By the end of the 19th century, millions of immigrants had arrived in America seeking a better life. But, all too often, what they found was poverty and deplorable living and working conditions in the tenement districts of large cities, none more oppressive than New York's Lower East Side. For seven days a week, 12 hours a day,

---

LABOR DAY

Labor Day, which is celebrated today on the first Monday in September, began in 1882 as a protest. In that year, the New York City Central Labor Council (NYCCLC), part of the Knights of Labor, called a march on September 5 (a Tuesday) to support the adoption of an eight-hour work day. When the Knights of Labor disbanded, the American Federation of Labor, headed by Samuel Gompers, embraced the idea of celebrating Labor Day. The Labor Day Parade in New York City and similar celebrations around the country continued without interruption. By 1894, several states and Congress had moved Labor Day to the first Monday in September, where it remains to this day.

To draw attention to the victims of child labor, two girls wear banners, in Yiddish and English, with the slogan ABOLISH CH[ILD] SLAVERY. *(Library of Congress, Prints and Photographs Division, LC-USZ62-22198)*

workers—mostly women—sewed clothing in sweatshops, in dark, filthy, crowded conditions. Paid only five cents for sewing the sleeves on a dozen blouses, the workers earned only $4 to $5 a week. But they took home even less because they actually had to pay for the thread and needles, the power to run the sewing machine, the chair they sat on, and the locker where they kept their personal belongings.

By the beginning of the 20th century, the conditions for workers hardly improved. Safety was of little or no concern to the owners. More than 130 people died in workplace fires every year. Unsanitary conditions caused disease at work and at home. Amid such inhumane circumstances, some brave workers found the time and courage to meet and organize, hoping to bring public attention to their plight. City officials, some of whom were accepting bribes from shop owners, were of no help. The workers had to do it themselves.

THE TRIANGLE SHIRTWAIST FIRE

On Saturday, March 25, 1911, the deadliest workplace disaster in New York City occurred on the ninth floor of the Triangle Shirtwaist factory in Lower Manhattan. The fire killed 146 people, who either jumped to their death trying to escape or were burned behind doors locked by the owners to prevent theft. The immigrant workers were mostly Jewish and Italian women in their teens and twenties struggling to make a meager living.

The fire and the devastating loss of life shocked the nation. Within days, 350,000 people joined in a huge funeral march, while another 250,000 lined the route. The public was appalled to learn what the workers had known all along: None of the factories in New York had sprinklers, firewalls, or fireproof doors, even though such safeguards were available.

Although the powerful New York Democratic Party machine known as Tammany Hall helped the owners of the Triangle factory win an acquittal on criminal charges and initially blocked reform legislation, soon young Democratic politicians, including future Governor Alfred E. Smith and future Senator Robert F. Wagner, were elected to the state legislature and actively supported reforms in working conditions that would eventually lead to FDR's New Deal.

On November 22, 1909, 15,000 shirtwaist workers, almost all women, went on strike, and the next day another 5,000 joined them. It was an extraordinary show of solidarity, and it attracted wide support from many quarters including suffragists, college students, social workers, and wealthy "society women," including the daughter of influential banker J. P. Morgan, as well as Frances Perkins, who would later become the first woman to serve as Secretary of Labor under President Franklin D. Roosevelt.

The "Uprising of the Twenty Thousand," as it was called, continued until the following February, but the strikers could not hold out any longer. Many were arrested, and once again the courts sided with the owners, who made slight concessions but refused to recognize the local union as the legitimate bargaining agent on behalf of all the workers.

RESTRAINING UNIONS

World War I ended in November 1918, and in the postwar economy, workers could not find jobs. Those who were employed had to work under unsafe and oppressive conditions, bringing home such paltry wages that they could not feed their families. Major strikes occurred in Seattle, Boston, Chicago, Knoxville, Tennessee, and Omaha, Nebraska, disrupting production and in some cases sparking violent reactions, prompting federal troops to halt the strikes and restore order.

In May 1920, authorities in Duquesne, Pennsylvania, responded to a demonstration that was sponsored by a new organization known as the American Civil Liberties Union (ACLU) in support of steel workers. The authorities went to court and obtained an injunction prohibiting *all* union meetings. In 1923, renowned author Upton Sinclair was arrested at a rally in San Pedro, California, in support of striking members of the Industrial Workers of the World (IWW, or the "Wobblies"). His crime was reading the First Amendment.

One of the most potent weapons used to block freedom of assembly was the injunction against union meetings. An injunction is a court order used to keep things as they are (maintaining the "status quo") until the court can hold a trial. In the 1920s and 1930s, injunctions were used to prevent unions from holding meetings or strikes. The injunctions had a devastating impact on unions, interfering with their ability to gather their members together to take collective action. Employers could obtain injunctions without proving that the union had engaged in any illegal or violent activity. In fact, in 1921, the U.S. Supreme Court upheld restrictions on peaceful picketing (marching in front of a factory or store and urging customers not to do business with the company), merely based on the speculation that picketing would "inevitably lead to intimidation and violence."

In 1924, 8,000 silk workers went on strike in Paterson, New Jersey. The mill owners eventually received fifteen injunctions that effectively prevented all union activity. The founder and head of the ACLU, Roger Baldwin, was appalled and organized a demonstration

Miners in Latrobe, Pennsylvania, go out on strike and march through the city to protest low wages and unsafe working conditions. *(Library of Congress, Prints and Photographs Division, LC-USZ62-23689)*

and march to City Hall. When Baldwin rose to speak to the rally, he was arrested and convicted of violating an "unlawful assembly" law dating back to 1796. Remarkably, New Jersey's highest court unanimously reversed Baldwin's conviction in a decision that represents one of the earliest endorsements of freedom of assembly (and freedom of speech). Citing the Magna Carta and other historic documents, the decision boldly held that both the New Jersey and U.S. Constitutions, "being in favor of liberty of the people, must be given the most liberal and comprehensive construction."

SUPREME COURT UPHOLDS FREEDOM OF ASSEMBLY

Legislative successes did not prevent some local authorities from continuing to violate the workers' rights. And no one was more abusive than the mayor of Jersey City, Frank Hague. Eager to attract business to his city, Hague actively suppressed labor unions by arbitrarily denying them meeting permits and authorizing the police to harass pickets. These actions were directed primarily at the new Congress of Industrial Organizations (CIO). In 1937, when Hague banned all CIO leaflets and rejected meeting requests from the ACLU and the Socialist Party, the ACLU decided to take the offensive and sued to prevent Hague from violating the First Amendment rights of union activists.

In 1938, in a stunning victory, the U.S. District Court ordered Jersey City to stop evicting union organizers from the city, to end illegal searches and seizures, and to cease interfering with meetings and the distribution of literature.

In 1939, the U.S. Supreme Court in *Hague v. CIO* issued a landmark opinion upholding freedom of assembly. The court called

NORRIS–LA GUARDIA AND WAGNER ACTS

In 1932, the cause of freedom of assembly and association enjoyed another victory, when Congress passed the Norris-La Guardia Act, restricting labor injunctions. The law, which Felix Frankfurter, a Harvard law school professor and future justice of the Supreme Court, helped write, declared that workers had a right to "full freedom of association, self-organization . . . [and] to be free from the interference, restraint, or coercion of employers." Under the law, injunctions could only be granted based on evidence of actual violence or substantial harm to the employer.

The Norris–La Guardia Act was a major step forward for those who advocated freedom of assembly and association. No longer could these rights be arbitrarily violated by sweeping injunctions that condemned unions before they had done anything illegal or violent.

Three years later, in 1935, Congress passed the Wagner Act, ensuring workers the right to organize unions "of their own choosing." Protection for unions to organize included the right to assemble and associate. The Wagner Act put an end to the days of local police disrupting union meetings.

"[W]herever the title of streets and parks may rest, they have immemorially been held in trust for the use of the public and, time out of mind, have been used for purposes of assembly, communicating thoughts between citizens, and discussing public questions."

—*Majority opinion, U.S. Supreme Court, Hague v. CIO, 1939*

WORKS PROGRESS ADMINISTRATION

The Works Progress Administration (WPA) was a relief measure established in 1935 by President Franklin D. Roosevelt. Headed by Harry L. Hopkins and funded with an initial congressional appropriation of $4,880,000,000, it offered work to the unemployed on an unprecedented scale by spending money on a wide variety of programs, including highway and building construction, slum clearance, reforestation, and rural rehabilitation.

The WPA included several innovative cultural programs that encouraged artists to work together for the betterment of society. The Federal Writers' Project created state and regional guidebooks, organized archives, indexed newspapers, and conducted sociological and historical investigations. The Federal Arts Project gave unemployed artists the opportunity to create art for hundreds of post offices, schools, and other public buildings with murals, canvases, and sculptures; musicians organized symphony orchestras and community singing. The Federal Theatre Project produced old and new plays, bringing drama to people who had never before seen a live theatrical production.

By March 1936, the WPA rolls had reached a total of more than 3,400,000 people; after initial cuts in June 1939, it averaged 2,300,000 monthly, and by June 30, 1943, when it was officially terminated, the WPA had employed more than 8,500,000 people on 1,410,000 individual projects and had spent about $11 billion. During its eight-year history, the WPA built 651,087 miles of highways, roads, and streets and constructed, repaired, or improved 124,031 bridges, 125,110 public buildings, 8,192 parks, and 853 airport landing fields.

Works Progress Administration (WPA) workers join in a mass meeting to protest congressional cuts in relief appropriations. *(Library of Congress, Prints and Photographs Division, LC-USF34-018930-E)*

streets and parks a "public forum" protected by the First Amendment. The very next year, in *Thornhill v. Alabama,* the Supreme Court ruled that the First Amendment protected peaceful picketing.

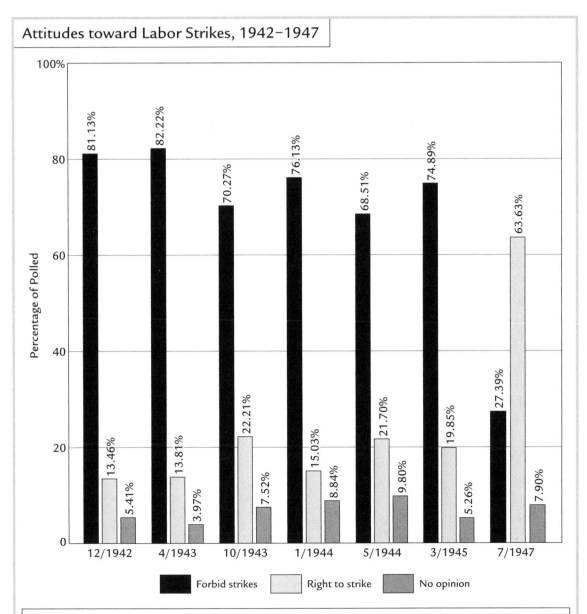

Attitudes toward Labor Strikes, 1942–1947

The above graph indicates public attitude from 1942 to 1945 when asked: "Should Congress pass a law forbidding strikes in war industries, or should workers in war industries continue to have the right to go on strike?" It also indicates public attitude in 1947 when asked: "Should Congress pass a law forbidding strikes in all industries, or should workers have the right to go on strikes?"
Source: Gallup Organization Polls—December 1942, April 1943, October 1943, January 1944, May 1944, March 1945, and July 1947.

During wartime, most people believe that everyone should pull together to support the war effort. During World War II, overwhelming majorities supported laws forbidding the right of employees to strike. After the war, opinions changed and almost two-thirds of Americans supported the right to strike.

The combination of *Hague* and *Thornhill* laid a solid constitutional foundation for freedom of assembly. Time and again down through the years, these decisions would be cited in hundreds of subsequent cases to uphold the right of people to peaceably assemble in public.

THE RISE OF UNIONISM

In the early 1940s, unions enjoyed significant growth in their membership. Between June 1940 and December 1941, the combined membership of the AFL and CIO increased by 1.5 million. Between 1939 and 1944, the membership of the United Automobile Workers (UAW) increased from 165,000 to more than 1 million; the shipbuilders' union went from 35,000 members to 209,000; the United Steelworkers of America grew from 450,000 members to 700,000; and the United Packinghouse Workers increased its membership from 39,000 to 100,000.

Given the sacrifices workers had made when wages were limited during World War II, they were not prepared when employers started cutting wages after the war ended. Union workers across the country called several strikes to try to increase their pay and improve their living standards.

Union workers complained that employers had earned enormous profits during the war and could easily afford to increase wages. In November 1945, 180,000 UAW members struck General Motors (GM) for higher wages but also insisted that GM not raise the prices of its cars to cover the cost of higher wages. In January 1946, 500,000 members of the United Steelworkers, 200,000 members of the United Electrical Workers, and 150,000 Packinghouse workers struck for higher pay. This round of strikes prompted up to 20 percent wage increases.

Some employers and conservative politicians tried to impede the progress of the movement. In 1947, Congress passed the Taft-Hartley Act, which made it illegal for unions to give money to political campaigns and outlawed "secondary boycotts" against a company that handled goods produced by another employer involved in a labor dispute. Taft-Hartley also outlawed sympathy strikes and "wildcat strikes," which are strikes that are not officially sanctioned by the union.

The Taft-Hartley Act also contained a controversial provision that required union officers to sign an affidavit that they did not belong to the Communist Party. The requirement divided the organization between those who feared communist influence in the labor movement and those who believed that one's political affiliation should not have anything to do with their right to join a labor union. In 1949, after bitter internal fights, the CIO expelled 11 unions whose officers refused to sign the affidavits.

The Taft-Hartley Act generated widespread opposition among working people. In Iowa, 100,000 workers stayed away from work in April 1947 to protest the law, and nearly 50,000 workers attended a rally at the state capitol in Des Moines to protest a proposed right-to-work bill.

Labor Movement in the 1970s and Beyond

The emergence of an antiunion atmosphere in the 1970s and 1980s hurt the labor movement. In 1970, more than 27 percent of all the workers in the United States were members of unions. But those numbers dropped steadily over the next 20 years. The membership of the United Steelworkers of America declined from more than 1 million in 1975 to less than 500,000 by 1987. The United Automobile Workers union lost 500,000 of its members in the late 1970s and early 1980s. Between 1975 and 1985, an antiunion campaign led by construction employers and an economic recession in the early 1980s reduced the proportion of construction workers who belonged to building trades unions from 65 percent to around 30 percent. By 1990, only 16 percent of all workers belonged to unions.

In August 1981, early in Ronald Reagan's presidency, 13,000 air traffic controllers employed by the government and members of the Professional Air Traffic Controllers' Organization (PATCO) went on strike for a better contract. Instead of negotiating with PATCO, President Reagan permanently replaced the union workers with nonunion controllers. Reagan's decision weakened the right to strike.

The 1990s saw an upsurge in union organizing. The AFL-CIO created its so-called Organizing Department with a $20 million budget and an Organizing Institute that recruited and trained union organizers.

In the 1990s, the Justice for Janitors campaign organized thousands of low-paid and mostly black and Latino janitors into unions.

"Don't scab for the bosses,
Don't listen to their lies.
Us poor folks haven't got a chance
Unless we organize.
Which side are you on?
Which side are you on?"

—Union folk song by Florence Reese, wife of a Kentucky miner, 1931

CESAR CHAVEZ

In every generation a new influx of immigrants has fueled the labor movement, seeking protection from exploitation and hoping for a better life. In the last part of the 20th century, immigrants from Mexico, South and Central America, and Asia joined immigrants from the rest of the world in this struggle.

In 1952, labor organizers, who wanted to unionize California workers who picked grapes, apricots, and other fruits and vegetables, discovered a 25-year-old farm worker outside San Jose named Cesar Chavez, who was dedicated to improving the lives of his coworkers and would lead that effort for the next 40 years.

In 1962, Chavez presided over the first convention of the National Farm Workers Association (NFWA). In 1966, Chavez led a 340-mile pilgrimage to the state capitol in Sacramento and organized a successful boycott of Schenley Vineyards, which resulted in the first genuine union contract between a grower and a farm workers' union in U.S. history.

In summer 1966, the NFWA and the Filipino American Agricultural Workers Organizing Committee merged to form the United Farm Workers (UFW). Over the next few years the UFW organized a nationwide grape boycott, which was highly successful in convincing grape growers and wineries to improve the wages and working conditions of farm laborers. In 1968, Senator Robert F. Kennedy of New York called Chavez "one of the heroic figures of our time."

As the UFW grew, it expanded its boycotts to other agricultural products, including lettuce. By 1975, a nationwide poll reported that 17 million Americans were boycotting grapes.

After Jerry Brown, a Democrat, was elected governor of California in 1975, he supported the formation of the Agricultural Labor Relations Board which protected the right of farm workers to organize. By the 1980s, more than 45,000 farm workers were protected by contracts negotiated by the UFW. When George Deukemejian, a Republican, was elected governor in 1982, he reduced the enforcement of the state's farm labor law. Farm workers lost their jobs, one was killed after voting in a union election, and Chavez mounted a third grape boycott.

In 1986, Chavez launched the "Wrath of Grapes" campaign (a play on words of John Steinbeck's novel *The Grapes of Wrath*), which publicized how grape workers and their children were being poisoned by pesticides used to kill insects that ruined grapevines.

On April 23, 1993, Cesar Chavez died at age 66. Forty thousand mourners attended his funeral. On August 8, 1994, President Bill Clinton posthumously awarded Chavez the Medal of Freedom, America's highest civilian honor. In 2003, Chavez was honored with a commemorative U.S. postage stamp.

Between 1990 and 1995, Justice for Janitors helped bring unions to 90 percent of the janitors in Los Angeles, won family medical benefits, and increased janitors' wages from $4.25 per hour to $6.80. Justice for Janitors organized unions among thousands of janitors in other major cities such as Philadelphia, San Diego, and Milwaukee. In Washington, D.C., in 1995, Justice for Janitors led demonstrations to protest cutbacks in welfare and education.

The labor movement has taken full advantage of the right to petition for redress of grievances. Members of unions regularly meet with their elected representatives in Congress, hold workshops on how to affect the political process, circulate petitions, and lead demonstrations. During elections, thousands of union members "get out the vote" for pro-labor candidates by distributing campaign literature, making phone calls, and talking to their coworkers. The AFL-CIO also lobbies politicians to support pro-worker legislation. It also provides resources to local unions and labor federations so they can educate union members about political issues and become effective political organizers.

On August 4, 1997, 180,000 United Parcel Service (UPS) employees stopped work and began the largest strike in the United States in 20 years. Workers across the country held rallies. UPS pilots stood in solidarity with the strikers and refused to fly packages. Fifteen days later, UPS agreed to create 10,000 new jobs, gave full-time employees a five-year, 15-percent raise, and gave the lower-paid, part-time workers a 37-percent raise.

The labor movement helped improve the lives of working men and women in America, protecting them from unsafe conditions, raising their wages, and increasing their benefits. The movement depended heavily on the active exercise of freedom of assembly, freedom of association, and the right to petition by millions of people. Only their united efforts ensured their success.

The Rights Revolution

THE ONGOING STRUGGLE FOR CIVIL AND WOMEN'S RIGHTS

By 1900, the oppression of blacks through slavery was replaced by the oppression of blacks through segregation. All southern states, in new constitutions and statutes, officially prevented African Americans from voting in state elections. In the North, 19 of the 24 states did not allow blacks to vote. Blacks would soon realize that it is one thing to pass constitutional amendments abolishing slavery, guaranteeing "due process" and "equal protection of the laws," and granting the right to vote, but it is quite another to actually eliminate racism from the minds and hearts of the people.

For many newly freed blacks, slavery was replaced by "wage slavery." The average pay for a black farm laborer in the South was about 50 cents a day, for 12 hours of backbreaking work. In his book *Black Reconstruction* (1935), W. E. B. DuBois, a prominent black writer, wrote that "there began to rise in America in 1876, a new capitalism and a new enslavement of labor."

MONTGOMERY BUS BOYCOTT

The modern civil rights movement spanning the second half of the 20th century was infused with historic marches, rallies, boycotts, sit-ins, and demonstrations. It was an extraordinary exercise of the rights of assembly, association, and petition.

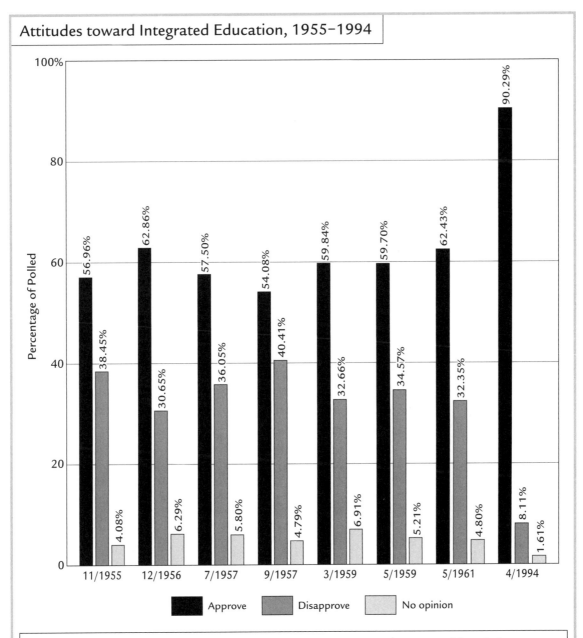

Attitudes toward Integrated Education, 1955–1994

Percentage of Polled

Date	Approve	Disapprove	No opinion
11/1955	56.96%	38.45%	4.08%
12/1956	62.86%	30.65%	6.29%
7/1957	57.50%	36.05%	5.80%
9/1957	54.08%	40.41%	4.79%
3/1959	59.84%	32.66%	6.91%
5/1959	59.70%	34.57%	5.21%
5/1961	62.43%	32.35%	4.80%
4/1994	90.29%	8.11%	1.61%

■ Approve   ▨ Disapprove   ▢ No opinion

The above graph indicates public attitude when asked: "Do you approve or disapprove of the U.S. Supreme Court decision in *Brown v. Board of Education* (1954) that all children, no matter their race, must be allowed to go to the same schools?"
Source: Gallup Organization Polls—November 1955, December 1956, July 1957, September 1957, March 1959, May 1959, May 1961, and April 1994.

When the U.S. Supreme Court decided *Brown v. Board of Education* in 1954, ordering an end to racial segregation in public schools, only slightly more than half the population approved. Year by year, support for school integration steadily grew.

"One of the great glories of democracy is the right to protest for right."

—*Martin Luther King, Jr., 1955*

On December 1, 1955, Rosa Parks, a 43-year-old seamstress from Montgomery, Alabama, defied the law by refusing to sit in the back of the bus in the segregated area set aside for blacks. Parks was arrested.

The outrage that followed gave vent to the anger and frustration among blacks (and their white supporters) who had lived far too long in a segregated society. A boycott of the city bus service was immediately organized by a group of black ministers and others in the name of the Montgomery Improvement Association (MIA). They recruited the new pastor of the Dexter Avenue Baptist Church, a 26-year-old minister named Martin Luther King, Jr., to lead their effort.

The next day, King spoke at a mass meeting at Holt Street Baptist Church. He urged his audience that if they "will protest courageously and yet with dignity and Christian love, when the history books are written in future generations the historians will pause and say 'There lived a great people—a black people—who injected new meaning and dignity into the veins of civilization.' That is our challenge and our overwhelming responsibility." For the next 13 years, King would lead a monumental, peaceful, and nonviolent struggle that would transform America.

The Montgomery boycott and mass meetings continued week after week, growing larger everyday. MIA organized a car-pool system so blacks could get to work. To try to defeat the boycott, Montgomery officials convened a grand jury, which on February 21, 1956, indicted 89 boycott leaders, including King and 23 other ministers. Their trial gained wide public attention. King was convicted and fined $1,000. The arrest made him a nationally known civil rights champion.

In June, Rosa Parks and four other women who had challenged the constitutionality of bus segregation won their case in federal district court. But in November, the city retaliated by obtaining a restraining order to prevent blacks from waiting on street corners for their car pools, on the grounds they were a "public nuisance."

That very same day, the U.S. Supreme Court upheld the decision in Parks's case striking down bus segregation. This was a major victory for racial equality and the right of people to peaceably assemble and associate together, without being subjected to discrimination.

The Montgomery bus boycott was not only successful in its own right, but it led to the formation of the Southern Christian Leadership Conference (SCLC), which elected King as its first president. It also demonstrated how the black community could organize and mobilize itself to fight for racial justice.

STUDENT SIT-INS

On February 1, 1960, four black students from North Carolina Agricultural and Technical College in Greensboro walked into a local Woolworth's department store and sat down at the segregated lunch counter, which was reserved for "whites only." They ordered coffee, and when they were refused service, they remained seated until the store closed.

The tactic of the "sit-in" was born, and it spread to other cities. In Tennessee, the Nashville Student Movement began a series of sit-ins. The students had been trained in nonviolence by James Lawson, a young black minister serving as the southern field secretary of the Fellowship of Reconciliation (FOR), an interracial pacifist group. Lawson became a powerful voice for nonviolent resistance, having studied the philosophy of Indian leader and pacifist Mohandas Gandhi. Lawson worked with King to strengthen nonviolence as a key component of the civil rights struggle.

The Nashville Student Movement organized 200 people to sit-in at major stores throughout the city. On February 27, 1960, a group of young whites pulled the black students from their lunch-counter seats and beat them. Instead of arresting the assailants, the Nashville police arrested the black protesters, charging them with "disorderly conduct."

For every student who was arrested, however, more arrived to take their place. With dignity and perseverance, the students would not be deterred. Eventually, in March, several students at the Greyhound bus terminal (a formerly whites-only establishment) were served, finally breaking the pattern of segregation.

On April 15, 1960, SCLC convened a conference on student sit-ins at Shaw University in Raleigh, North Carolina. Hoping for 100, instead 300 students turned out and were joined by Lawson, who had been expelled from Vanderbilt's divinity school for encouraging the Nashville students to participate in the sit-ins. As an

CIVIL DISOBEDIENCE

A powerful form of nonviolent protest is called civil disobedience. Activists deliberately violate the law and accept the consequences by going to jail or paying a fine to bring attention to their cause. Sometimes the focus of the protest is the law that is being broken. Other times activists block traffic or trespass on government property to protest another law or a broader government policy.

An early proponent of civil disobedience, which he called passive resistance, was Mohandas Gandhi, born in 1869 to Hindu parents in India. After studying law in England, Gandhi worked tirelessly in South Africa to improve the rights of immigrant Indians. Gandhi was frequently arrested. He said that "nonviolence is the greatest force at the disposal of mankind. It is mightier than the mightiest weapon of destruction devised by the ingenuity of man."

Back in India, Gandhi spent the next 30 years protesting English colonial rule. He was deeply dedicated to nonviolence and passive resistance and gained worldwide stature as a peacemaker. In January 1948, he was assassinated at the age of 79.

In the United States, the practice of civil disobedience is traced to author Henry David Thoreau, who wrote "On the Duty of Civil Disobedience." He engaged in the classic form of civil disobedience by refusing to pay taxes to support what he considered an imperialistic war with Mexico. Thoreau was a writer, philosopher, and naturalist. Regarding civil disobedience he asked: "Unjust laws exist: shall we be content to obey them, or shall we endeavor to amend them, and obey them until we have succeeded, or shall we transgress them at once?" Thoreau declared that under "a government which imprisons any unjustly, the true place for a just man is also in prison."

Later in the 20th and 21st centuries, the civil rights, labor, women's, antinuclear, and antiwar movements all used peaceful civil disobedience to promote their cause. Images of protesters joining arms, sitting in the street, and blocking traffic, in acts of nonviolent civil disobedience, are indelibly etched in the minds of people who have lived through these movements. Civil disobedience represents one of the purest exercises of freedom of assembly.

outgrowth of the conference, the Student Nonviolent Coordinating Committee (SNCC, pronounced "snick") was formed.

Two days after the conference, the home of a Nashville city councilman who had supported the sit-ins was bombed. In response, the Nashville Student Movement organized a march to City Hall. Never before had as many as 2,500 students and supporters marched peacefully in silence. When a representative of the marchers confronted the mayor and asked if he thought it was wrong to discriminate against someone on the basis of their race or color, the mayor nodded and said he did.

This was a critical success for the movement and proved the power of peaceful, concerted action. By October 1960, sit-ins had taken place in 112 southern cities. The combined effort of so many people, in several different locations, reinforced the strength of the movement.

The power of these marches and sit-ins came from the unquenchable supply of protesters willing to be arrested in the cause of civil rights. Every new wave of students showed that the authorities would never win.

FREEDOM RIDES

In summer 1961, the Congress of Racial Equality (CORE), originally founded in 1942, began organizing "freedom rides" into the South. The program was intended to force compliance with a recent U.S. Supreme Court decision that upheld the integration of bus stations and terminals involved in interstate travel. Blacks sat in the front of the bus, while whites sat in the back. At stops along the way, whites entered the waiting rooms marked "Colored," and blacks used the whites-only facilities.

The first freedom ride left Washington, D.C., on May 4, 1961, with 13 riders. The freedom rides gained national and international attention, revealing the stark contrast between peaceful black and white riders exercising their constitutional rights and unruly racists violently resisting integration. Over the course of the summer, almost 400 riders participated in this effort, most of whom were arrested and jailed.

On December 10, 1961, 10 freedom riders were arrested in Atlanta, Georgia, on grounds of "trespassing." The next day, 267 students from Albany State College and the local black high school marched to the train station, where they too were arrested. The following day, 200 more protesters marched to city hall and they were all arrested.

With more than 500 protesters arrested, Dr. King arrived in Atlanta to show his support. When King led 265 demonstrators on a march from a church to city hall, most of them, including King, were arrested. After his release, King announced another march, but the city got a restraining order preventing him and his supporters from going forward.

Four days later, a federal appeals court overturned the injunction, and the next day 2,000 blacks marched through the streets of Atlanta, protesting the arrests and the segregationist policies of the city.

Civil rights activists organized by the Congress on Racial Equality (CORE) march in protest against slum housing. *(Library of Congress, Prints and Photographs Division, LC-USZ62-115077)*

PROTESTS IN BIRMINGHAM

On April 3, 1963, civil rights leaders led by Dr. King launched Project C (for "Confrontation") in Birmingham, Alabama's largest city with a black population of 350,000, representing 40 percent of the city. The protesters marched, sang, and prayed. Three days later, during another march, 30 demonstrators were arrested.

In reaction to Project C, the Birmingham police commissioner convinced an Alabama state judge to enjoin King and 132 other civil rights leaders from taking part or encouraging any more marches, sit-ins, protests, or other demonstrations. King defied the blatantly unconstitutional order and on Good Friday led a march of 50 demonstrators. He was promptly arrested and placed in solitary confinement.

The *Birmingham News* published a full-page open letter from eight local white clergymen criticizing King for the demonstrations. In response, King wrote what would become known as his famous "Letter from a Birmingham Jail." In it, King wrote that "freedom is never voluntarily given by the oppressor; it must be demanded by the oppressed."

THE MARCH ON WASHINGTON

On August 28, 1963, the March on Washington, one of the most momentous exercises of freedom of assembly in American history, brought 250,000 people to the nation's capital in the cause of civil rights. Organized by the NAACP, the Congress of Racial Equality (CORE), SNCC, the United Auto Workers, the National Catholic Conference for Interracial Justice, the American Jewish Congress, the International Ladies Garment Workers Union, the Union of Electrical Workers, the Communication Workers of America, and the Brotherhood of Sleeping Car Porters, the massive demonstration brought together blacks and whites in a peaceful and outspoken call for justice and equal rights.

Beginning at the Washington Monument, where entertainers such as Sidney Poitier, Charlton Heston, Marlon Brando, Paul Newman, Burt Lancaster, Harry Belafonte, Joan Baez, and Peter, Paul, and Mary performed for the crowd, the march proceeded one mile to the Lincoln Monument. There, with the Voice of America broadcasting the historic event around the world, Dr. King delivered his famous "I Have a Dream" speech.

"We can't tolerate the NAACP or the Student Nonviolent Committee or any other nigger organizations to take over this town with mass demonstrations."

—Police Chief Laurie Pritchett, 1960

"I dream that one day all of God's children—black men and white men, Jews and Gentiles, Protestants and Catholics—will be able to join hands and sing in the words of the old Negro spiritual, 'Free at last, free at last, thank God Almighty, we are free at last.'"

—Dr. Martin Luther King, Jr., 1963

The impact of the 1963 March on Washington cannot be overstated. It was a galvanizing event for the civil rights movement, placing it front and center on the nation's agenda. The sheer size of the demonstration prevented it from being dismissed as a marginal "fringe" event. To this day, the march is remembered as one of the single-largest outpourings of unity and solidarity on any political or social issue. And it symbolizes the power of collective action in service of freedom of assembly and association.

FREEDOM SUMMER

The summer of 1964 became known as "Freedom Summer" as hundreds of volunteers organized by the Council of Federated Organizations (COFO), a coalition of civil rights organizations, including the NAACP, SNCC, SCLC, and CORE, fanned out through Mississippi in a massive voter-registration drive. Eight hundred students were trained not only in the rules of voter eligibility but also in peaceful nonviolence.

To challenge the entrenched all-white Democratic Party, SNCC formed the Mississippi Freedom Democratic Party (MFDP). To everyone's surprise, the energetic Freedom Summer volunteers recruited 80,000 blacks and many whites to join MFDP. That was a huge number of voters and posed a genuine threat to the establishment. On August 6, 1964, 2,500 people attended MFDP's first state convention and chose 64 blacks and four whites as delegates to the Democratic National Convention. The formation of the MFDP was a bold exercise of freedom of association.

With racial tensions boiling under the surface and from time to time erupting in violence, it took great courage to oppose the system. In fact, on June 21, 1964, three young civil rights workers—Andrew Goodman, James Chaney, and Michael Schwerner—disappeared while in Mississippi. Six weeks later their bodies were found riddled with .38-caliber bullets. Twenty-one whites, including a deputy sheriff, were taken into custody in connection with the murders, but state charges were dropped. Six were later convicted in federal court and sent to prison for violating the civil rights of the three young men.

What is sometimes overlooked is that the March on Washington was also a vast exercise of the right to petition the government for redress of grievances. Despite the fact that for many the word *petition* conjures up a written document bearing numerous signatures, there are many ways to petition the government to correct injustice. The March on Washington was one of them. Held in the seat of national government, every one of the 250,000 people who attended registered a personal plea—a petition—that the federal government had to act to enforce the Constitution and protect equal rights.

The government received the message. On July 2, 1964, President Lyndon Johnson signed the historic Civil Rights Act of 1964, prohibiting discrimination in public accommodations, which President John F. Kennedy had submitted to Congress before his tragic assassination on November 22, 1963.

SELMA, ALABAMA

The small city of Selma, Alabama, became the center of the voting rights campaign. With a population of 30,000 evenly divided between blacks and whites, 65 percent of whites were registered to vote compared to only 1 percent of blacks.

In 1963, when SNCC arranged for voter-registration meetings within the black community, the sheriff harassed them. When SNCC workers arrived at the courthouse, they were arrested. What SNCC saw as lawful acts of assembly, association, and petition were being blocked by government officials.

On January 2, 1965, Dr. King, having just received the prestigious Nobel Peace Prize, arrived in Selma to support the voting rights struggle. He spoke in Brown's Chapel of the African Methodist Episcopal Church to a large crowd of 700 people. A few weeks later, SCLC began daily marches to the courthouse. When the sheriff attacked a young woman, it was reported in the national news.

A few days later, 100 black schoolteachers marched to the courthouse to protest the arrest and mistreatment of the young woman. The sight of respected middle-class teachers protesting had significant impact. One civil rights leader called it the most important civil rights action since the original Montgomery bus boycott more than a decade earlier.

On February 1, King spoke to 250 marchers at a church and then led them to the courthouse where they were all arrested, together with the 500 schoolchildren who followed them. To dramatize the plight of blacks, King released a statement pointing out that in Selma, Alabama, "THERE ARE MORE NEGROES IN JAIL WITH ME THAN THERE ARE ON THE VOTING ROLLS."

Within days, President Johnson announced that he was sending a voting rights bill to Congress. The peaceful actions of protesters compared to the brutal, repressive tactics of the authorities had made an impact on the American public and reached the highest level of government.

King and others announced that on March 7, 1965, there would be a march from Selma to Montgomery, the state capitol. Alabama Governor George Wallace, an avowed segregationist, announced that there would be no such march because it could tie up traffic on the highway.

In a remarkable show of support, the day before the march, 70 local white citizens assembled on the steps of the county courthouse, where they announced that they wanted the nation to know that there were white people in Alabama who opposed the brutal way the police were interfering with peaceful demonstrations of people who were simply exercising their constitutional rights.

The next day, 600 people gathered for the march to Montgomery. As they approached the Edmund Pettus Bridge, they were met by Alabama state troopers, who ordered the marchers to turn back. While the leaders of the march tried to talk to the official in charge, the troops pushed and clubbed anyone in their way and fired tear gas. Television broadcast live scenes of the state troopers trampling peaceful protesters.

The following day, Dr. King led 1,500 marchers along the same route toward the bridge. Again, they were confronted by state troopers. This time King knelt down in front of the troopers and led the protesters in prayer.

A week after the first march, President Johnson submitted a Voting Rights Act to a joint session of Congress, saying that he was speaking for "the dignity of man and the destiny of democracy." Referring specifically to Selma, President Johnson called on all Americans to "overcome the crippling legacy of bigotry and injustice. And we shall overcome. We *shall* overcome!"

The next day, a federal judge ruled that SCLC had a constitutional right to march from Selma to Montgomery. The judge found that a "pattern of harassment, intimidation, coercion, threatening conduct and, sometimes, brutal mistreatment" had been used by authorities to prevent blacks "from exercising their rights of citizenship, particularly the right to register to vote and the right to demonstrate peaceably for the purpose of protesting discriminatory practices."

In those concluding words, the judge described what the decade-long—indeed, centuries-long—civil rights struggle had been about: To protest segregation and the lasting legacy of slavery, blacks had taken seriously the guarantees of the First Amendment. Again, as the judge put it, they had "the right to demonstrate peaceably for the purpose of protesting discriminatory practices."

Despite killings, beatings, arrests, and harassment, by remaining true to the Constitution the civil rights movement prevailed. It gained the support of the majority of the American people. It secured redress for the grievances of racism, discrimination, and inequality through the passage of the Civil Rights Act of 1964 and the Voting Rights Act of 1965.

The civil rights movement hardly succeeded in gaining full equality for all people of color. Much work remained to be done. There would be setbacks and reversals. But there was no turning back.

THE EQUAL RIGHTS AMENDMENT

Amending the Constitution to add the Nineteenth Amendment guaranteeing women the right to vote did not automatically mend a society still infected by sexism and gender discrimination. In 1923, at the celebration of the 75th anniversary of the 1848 Woman's Rights Convention, Alice Paul introduced the Lucretia Mott Amendment, which read: "Men and women shall have equal rights throughout the United States and every place subject to its jurisdiction." The Equal Rights Amendment (ERA) would be introduced in every session of Congress until it passed in 1972. Yet it would never be ratified by the required number of states.

The National Woman's Party and others actively supported the amendment. But reformers who sought "protective" labor laws that treated women differently from men feared that the ERA would actually be harmful to women.

GAY RIGHTS MOVEMENT

While people of color and women largely fought their battles for equal rights in the glare of public scrutiny, gay, lesbian, bisexual, and transgendered persons (GLBT) were hidden from public view for most of American history due to severe hostility and recriminations exhibited by the majority of Americans. The GLBT community became more visible after World War II, only to be met by purges and firings from government jobs and the military. In 1953, President Dwight D. Eisenhower issued an executive order barring gay men and lesbians from holding any federal job.

In the early 1950s, some gays in Los Angeles began to organize and formed the Mattachine Society. It was joined in 1955 by a lesbian organization in San Francisco, the Daughters of Bilitis. These groups formed chapters in several cities. They afforded people who had been marginalized by society a place to meet and associate.

In the 1960s, what the participants called the "homophile movement" became more active, energized by the broader civil rights movement. Activists picketed governmental agencies in Washington, D.C., to protest discriminatory employment policies. By 1969, there were approximately 50 different homophile organizations in the United States. Friday, June 27, 1969, was a pivotal date in the GLBT movement. That night New York City police raided a gay bar in Greenwich Village called the Stonewall Inn. Instead of quietly accepting yet another incident of police harassment, gays and lesbians fought back, prompting three confrontational nights dubbed the "Stonewall Riots." Never again would the GLBT movement remain behind closed doors.

In 1970, 5,000 gay men and lesbians marched in New York City to commemorate the first anniversary of the Stonewall Riots. By 1973, there were almost 800 gay and lesbian organizations, including the Gay Liberation Front and Gay Activists' Alliance. The first gay rights march in the United States was held in Washing-

In the early 1940s, the Republican Party and later the Democratic Party supported the Equal Rights Amendment. The ERA was revised in 1943 to read: "Equality of rights under the law

ton, D.C., on October 14, 1979, with an estimated turnout of approximately 100,000 people. As the GLBT movement grew, new organizations emerged, including the Human Rights Campaign, the National Gay and Lesbian Task Force, Parents and Friends of Lesbians and Gays, and the Gay and Lesbian Alliance Against Defamation.

Beginning in the early 1980s, the gay community was devastated by the AIDS epidemic. Now the movement was a matter of life and death. Antigay rhetoric, which had gained public attention in episodes such as singer Anita Bryant's 1977 campaign to repeal a gay rights ordinance in Dade County, Florida, intensified during the AIDS crisis. The movement reacted by expanding its political reach, demanding funding for AIDS research and education and greater protection against discrimination. In 1987, more than 600,000 marched on Washington to demand equality. By 1989, having boldly exercised their freedom of assembly and freedom of association, the GLBT movement was changing minds and expanding equality.

The struggle for equal rights for GLBT persons ran into deeply held values over the right of same-sex couples to marry. In 1996, Congress passed the Defense of Marriage Act restricting the federal definition of marriage to heterosexual couples. In 1999, the Vermont Supreme Court declared that the state must grant homosexual couples the same rights and protections that married heterosexuals enjoyed, and the Vermont Legislature authorized "civil unions" for same-sex couples. In 2003, Massachusetts's highest court ruled that homosexual couples have a constitutional right to marry. In June 2003 in *Lawrence v. Texas,* the U.S. Supreme Court overturned an antisodomy law and extended the right of privacy to consensual adult homosexual and heterosexual acts. In 2004, President George W. Bush called for an amendment to the U.S. Constitution prohibiting same-sex marriages, prompting renewed protests over the latest group seeking equal rights.

shall not be denied or abridged by the United States or by any state on account of sex." But it still did not gain a majority in Congress.

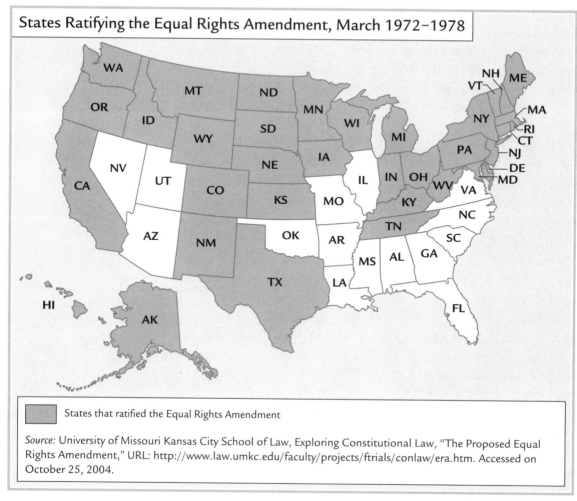

States Ratifying the Equal Rights Amendment, March 1972–1978

States that ratified the Equal Rights Amendment

Source: University of Missouri Kansas City School of Law, Exploring Constitutional Law, "The Proposed Equal Rights Amendment," URL: http://www.law.umkc.edu/faculty/projects/ftrials/conlaw/era.htm. Accessed on October 25, 2004.

Supporters of women's rights were optimistic when the Equal Rights Amendment was approved by Congress in 1972. All it would take to become part of the Constitution was ratification by 38 states. By 1978, only three states remained, but the required total was never achieved.

In the 1960s, the civil rights movement gave the ERA renewed energy. Women organized to demand their rights as citizens and persons. The Equal Rights Amendment became a lightning rod for the emerging feminist movement.

In 1972, the Equal Rights Amendment passed the U.S. Senate and the House of Representatives. On March 22, 1972, the proposed Twenty-seventh Amendment to the Constitution was sent to the states for ratification. To become law, a proposed amendment requires approval by three-fourths of the states.

Due to aggressive organizing, meetings, marches, and lobbying, the ERA quickly received 22 of the necessary 38 state ratifications in the first year. But as opposition grew, there were only eight ratifications in 1973, three in 1974, one in 1975, and none in 1976.

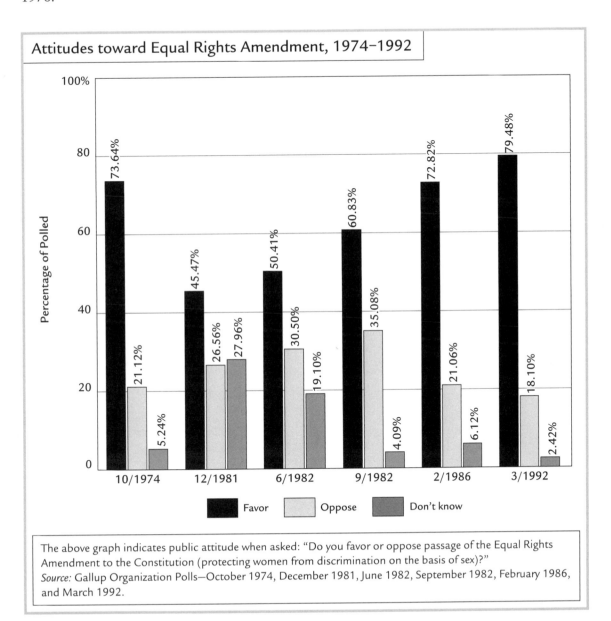

Attitudes toward Equal Rights Amendment, 1974–1992

Percentage of Polled

- Favor
- Oppose
- Don't know

The above graph indicates public attitude when asked: "Do you favor or oppose passage of the Equal Rights Amendment to the Constitution (protecting women from discrimination on the basis of sex)?"
Source: Gallup Organization Polls—October 1974, December 1981, June 1982, September 1982, February 1986, and March 1992.

Despite early support for the Equal Rights Amendment (almost 74 percent in 1974), opposition steadily grew. By the deadline for ratification in 1982, barely 50 percent supported the amendment.

The National Organization for Women (NOW) and ERAmerica, a coalition of nearly 80 mainstream organizations, staged rallies and marches in support of the ERA. Women were trying to use their rights of assembly and association to win ratification of the ERA. In 1977, Indiana became the 35th (and last) state to ratify the ERA. Illinois changed its rules to make it more difficult to ratify an amendment. Other states proposed or passed bills allowing them to take back a previous ratification, despite legal precedent that states do not have the power to retract a ratification.

As the 1979 deadline for ratification approached, ERA advocates appealed to Congress for an indefinite extension. In July 1978, NOW coordinated a massive march of 100,000 supporters in Washington, D.C., prompting Congress to grant an extension until June 30, 1982. It was a vast outpouring of support driven by a vast exercise of the right to assemble.

In 1980 the Republican Party removed the ERA from its platform. Pro-ERA efforts responded with massive lobbying, petitioning, rallies, hunger strikes, White House picketing, and civil disobedience. Despite these efforts, the ERA failed to get the three additional state ratifications needed before the deadline. Despite one of the longest and most sustained political efforts in American history, supported by the widespread exercise of freedom of assembly and outspoken protests, the country rejected incorporating a declaration of equal rights for women into the Constitution.

The Equal Rights Amendment was reintroduced in Congress on July 1, 1982, and has been before every session of Congress ever since. Women have made effective use of their freedom of assembly, freedom of association, and the right to petition government for redress of grievances. But like most social and political movements, much remains undone. The Nineteenth Amendment was clearly a major victory for women's rights, but the failure to ratify the ERA was a great disappointment.

5

World War I, World War II, and the Cold War

When most people think of freedom of assembly, they visualize political protesters marching in the street, rallying in large demonstrations, carrying signs and chanting slogans, speaking out for or against any number of causes and issues.

U.S. history is generously decorated with these public assemblies. They are the essence of free and open protest in a democratic society. Marches, demonstrations, and rallies are at the heart of freedom of assembly. Yet sometimes police and government officials have restricted or prohibited demonstrations and, on occasion, harassed, beaten, and even killed protesters in the name of protecting law and order.

WORLD WAR I

Twentieth-century America frequently found the forces of protest and authority in direct conflict. The rights of assembly, association, and petition were repeatedly tested. Also challenged were authorities' attempts to maintain the peace and protect the rights of citizens who were not protesting.

The United States entered World War I in April 1917. It first sent tens of thousands and eventually millions of young men to fight against Germany. Most Americans enthusiastically supported their country and would not tolerate anyone who did not. Critics of U.S. policy were treated as disloyal traitors, whose protests would undermine the war effort and demoralize the troops.

Within months after the start of World War I, on the Fourth of July, the *New York Times* editorialized that "freedom of speech" was certainly "well worth fighting for," but that in time of war "good citizens" willingly submit to limits on their rights to ensure "national existence and welfare" and if anyone insisted on protesting, the "jails are waiting for them."

In fact, at the time there was considerable opposition to the war among socialists, religious pacifists, German Americans, Irish Americans, Eastern European immigrants, and isolationists. Many of these opponents of the war also objected to the treatment of workers and other aspects of the American economic system. Many were recent immigrants, including Italians, Jews, and Eastern Europeans, who were the brunt of prejudice and discrimination. In that climate, many opponents of the war were attacked as being unpatriotic.

One of the earliest protests against the war, organized by anarchists Emma Goldman and Alexander Berkman on behalf of the

"No Conscription League," which opposed the involuntary draft of young men into the military, attracted a boisterous crowd of 8,000, leading to fights between pro-war and antiwar supporters. Anarchists opposed the concentration of power in any government, believing that inevitably all governments tend to oppress the people. During World War I, federal authorities were concerned that anarchists and other opponents of the war would spread disloyalty and encourage young men to refuse to be drafted into the military, thereby interfering with the war effort and the security of the United States. They were also concerned about anarchists' basic opposition to all government, and feared violent acts such as some that had occurred in Europe. After Goldman and Berkman organized two more tumultuous rallies, the federal government indicted them for "obstructing the draft" in violation of the Espionage Act, which Congress had enacted in June 1917. Lawyers for the anarchists argued that their clients were simply exercising their rights to assemble and their freedom of speech. The

For protesting against the military draft in World War I, Emma Goldman was convicted under the Espionage Act and deported to Russia. *(Library of Congress, Prints and Photographs Division, LC-USZ62-48418)*

POLITICAL DISSENT AND THE FBI

In 1919, the government agency that would become the Federal Bureau of Investigation (FBI) assigned a young clerk named J. Edgar Hoover to collect information on political dissidents. He quickly created secret files on more than 200,000 people, with detailed profiles on 60,000 of them, including pacifists, socialists, labor leaders, civil liberties advocates, and black activists. By 1921, Hoover had some 450,000 names in his files. More often than not, what qualified people for Hoover's secret files were their political views. Few had engaged in anything illegal, but their association with anyone considered suspicious was enough to get them on the FBI's list. This sort of guilt by association resulted in sweeping violations of the rights of assembly, association, and petition. People were considered guilty for belonging to organizations, attending meetings, or joining in peaceful protests. They were stigmatized as "enemies" of the United States. As a result, some were convicted and sent to jail.

Justice Department argued that these rallies and speeches were illegal because they might persuade young men not to enlist in the military. Goldman, Berkman, and others were convicted, imprisoned, and deported to the Soviet Union.

The Postwar Era

When the war ended, many workers could not find jobs, and others who were employed had to work under unsafe conditions or were paid such low wages that they could not feed their families. Labor organizers staged strikes to try and combat these problems. During this period, major strikes occurred in Seattle, Washington; Boston, Massachusetts; Chicago; Knoxville, Tennessee; and Omaha, Nebraska. They disrupted production and in some cases sparked violence. In many instances federal troops were brought in to halt the strikes and restore order.

The protesters and labor activists were not blameless for the ensuing violence. Some were intent on bringing about violent revolution. A series of bomb threats and deadly bombings occurred in various places in the United States, from Seattle to Georgia. Thirty-four mail bombs addressed to prominent Americans were discovered at a New York City post office. On June 2, 1919, bombs exploded in eight cities, killing a postman on the doorstep of Attorney General A. Mitchell Palmer.

Although these bombings and other acts of violence were committed by only a tiny fraction of protesters, they triggered widespread fear around the country. The public, already concerned about threats to the government by anarchists, communists, and others, feared a wave of killings and bloodshed. In this atmosphere, there was little tolerance of anyone who was critical of the government. Even those who were peaceful and nonviolent in their protests might be considered guilty by association.

Communist organizations began to form in the United States around 1919 to support the Bolshevik Revolution, which had happened two years prior in Russia. Czar Nicholas II had been removed from the throne in Russia and replaced by an interim government. In the face of widespread poverty and a disastrous economy, V. I. Lenin, a revolutionary, assumed leadership of the Bolshevik Party, which overthrew the government in 1917. In its place, the Soviet Union was established under the Communist Party. Communism is an economic system characterized by the collective ownership of property through the state, seeking a classless society. By contrast, under capitalism—the system of the United States—private parties own the means of production. In the early days of communism, their leaders believed there could be a worldwide revolution, converting all countries to communism.

In the United States for the next half century, the establishment and growth of the Communist Party (CP) would test the bounds of freedom of assembly, freedom of association, and the right to petition the government for redress of grievances. On the one hand, the U.S. government was deeply concerned that an international communist conspiracy was intent on overthrowing the established system in America (as it had done in Russia). On the other hand, many liberals and progressives in America found much to admire in communism, particularly its goals of ensuring racial equality and that workers enjoy the fruits of their labors with fair wages, safe working conditions, decent housing, complete medical care, and a good education for their children.

The tension between these two views would influence politics and law in the United States for decades. Among the questions that would have to be addressed: Did the Constitution protect the rights of communists to peaceably assemble and organize? Were communists as a group outside of the Constitution because their own political ideology sought the overthrow of the American system itself?

Soon the federal government and several states launched investigations into the threat of communism. Pacifists and critics of the war—whether or not they were members of the Communist Party—were often associated with communists and were condemned as subversives. Membership in certain organizations became a crime, even without any proof of a specific criminal or violent act, despite First Amendment protection for freedom of association.

The White House often serves as the site of protests; here, the wives and children of men convicted for their political activities gather. *(Library of Congress, Prints and Photographs Division, LC-USZ6-1820)*

Time and again the debate rages over preserving civil liberties during war and crisis. *(Library of Congress, Prints and Photographs Division, LC-USZC2-866)*

"There is no time to waste on hairsplitting over the infringement of liberty."

—Washington Post, *1920, commenting on violations of civil liberties during the Palmer Raids.*

According to Ellen Schrecker in her book *Many Are the Crimes: McCarthyism in America* (1998), commenting on the early days of the Communist Party especially during the Red Scare of 1919–20, "when the federal government rounded up thousands of foreign-born radicals for deportation, official repression forced the fledgling party underground."

The FBI, government officials, and many citizens believed the American Communist Party to be a grave threat to the United States. The American CP, as a member of the Comintern, the international communist organization established by Lenin in 1919, took orders from the Soviet Union. The American CP operated in secret and followed the dictates of a foreign power. The U.S. government feared that the CP was preparing to overthrow the American system as part of its worldwide revolution.

In November 1919, the FBI conducted coordinated raids in 12 different cities, arresting more than 250 men in what would become known as the Palmer Raids, named after the attorney general at the time, A. Mitchell Palmer. On January 2, 1920, the Justice Department expanded the raids in 33 cities, arresting more than 4,000 people. In most instances the arrests were lawless, that is, they were made without warrants. They were accompanied by unreasonable searches and seizures, destruction of personal property, physical brutality, and lengthy detentions. The guilt by association was so broad that anyone who looked "foreign" was rounded up.

At the time, though some viewed these government actions as abuses of freedom of assembly and association (not to mention freedom of speech and due process), the majority of the public and the mainstream press applauded what Attorney General Palmer had done. Today, however, the Palmer Raids are cited by historians as one of the most sweeping violations of civil liberties in American history.

Given the gravity of the abuses, some groups expressed outrage toward the government. The American Civil Liberties Union (ACLU), founded in 1920, and the National Popular Government League issued a paper titled *Report upon the Illegal Practices of the United States Department of Justice.* Signed by 12 prominent lawyers, including Felix Frankfurter, who would later serve as a U.S. Supreme Court justice, the report condemned the "utterly illegal acts which have been committed by those charged with the highest duty of enforcing the laws" and which "[have] struck at the foundation of American free institutions and have brought the name of our country into disrepute."

These sentiments were not widespread and failed to stop officials from continuing to conduct police raids on union meetings, deny speaking permits, and ignore mobs that attacked socialists, blacks, and union organizers. The ACLU documented police suppression of political meetings in 100 different cities.

In this same period, the Ku Klux Klan (KKK), a white supremacist organization that preached that blacks were inferior to whites, also attempted to exercise its rights of assembly and association. In 1923, Boston Mayor James Curley banned public meetings of the KKK. One KKK rally was attended by 300 Harvard students. The ACLU offered to defend the First Amendment rights of the KKK to peaceably assemble, despite the fact that the ACLU itself did not agree with the KKK's racist views. The KKK was also banned from holding public meetings in Wisconsin and Kansas.

A New York law that required registration and disclosure of the KKK's membership list was upheld by the U.S. Supreme Court in *Bryant v. Zimmerman* in 1928, in a decision that held that one type of organization could be regulated in one way but another type could not. The court's approach allowed judges to grant or withhold constitutional protection based on a judge's own biases and preconceptions of particular organizations, such as the KKK and the Communist Party.

Eugene Debs, socialist candidate for president on five occasions, leaves the federal penitentiary in Atlanta, Georgia, on Christmas Day, 1921, after serving a sentence for violating the Espionage and Sedition Acts. *(Library of Congress, Prints and Photographs Division, LC-USZ62-75579)*

NAZIS AND COMMUNISTS

Adolf Hitler, who founded the Nazi Party in Germany based on a theory of racial superiority, came to power in Germany in 1933. Groups sympathetic to Nazism began to form in the United States, including an organization known as the German-American *Bund,* which attracted thousands of people to pro-Nazi demonstrations in New York, New Jersey, Ohio, and Illinois. In 1937 at the Bund's Camp Nordland in New Jersey, more than 18,000 people marched in Nazi uniforms singing the Nazi anthem and saluting the Nazi flag. Once again the fundamental question facing the United States was whether its institutions, including the constitutional protections for the rights of assembly and association, were strong enough to protect a political party that, if it were in power, would not protect such freedoms for anyone else.

Meanwhile, by the mid-1930s, the American CP began to temper its revolutionary rhetoric and tried to broaden its appeal by organizing the Popular Front, to attract more mainstream liberals who were not members of the Communist Party. In 1935, the Seventh World Congress of the Comintern had encouraged local communist parties to create political coalitions with labor unions and other groups opposed to Nazism.

Fearing the rise of communism, the House of Representatives responded in 1938 by creating the House Un-American Activities Committee, popularly known as HUAC. The committee held numerous public hearings, alleging that there was Communist "influence" in labor unions and in various government agencies established under President Franklin Delano Roosevelt's (FDR) administration.

For the next 38 years, HUAC pursued a strategy of guilt by association. Though membership in the Communist Party was not a crime, HUAC acted as if it were. Sometimes even non-Communists who associated with the Communist Party, for example by giving money to a legal defense committee to defend Communists, were treated as Communists.

HUAC would compel those suspected of being Communists to appear before public hearings. In Chicago, Philadelphia, and Washington, D.C., HUAC raided the offices of left-wing groups, seizing their records and membership lists. This happened in an atmosphere of fear and when many Americans were scared that Communists would overthrow the government, take away their private property, and possibly even enslave them. Congress in 1938 passed the Smith Act, which made it a crime to advocate the overthrow of the government by force or violence and outlawed membership in any organization advocating such an overthrow.

The American CP had grown from 40,000 members in 1936 to 82,000 by the end of 1938. Some were federal civil servants and others held sensitive and important positions in the government. Others may well have been spies. Many government officials believed that every Communist was a potential spy whose true loyalty was to the Soviet Union, not the United States.

In 1939, President Franklin Roosevelt asked J. Edgar Hoover, now head of the FBI, to investigate Communists and other "subversive activities," giving the agency new and expansive authority to secretly look into political organizations, Communist and non-Communist alike. In 1940, Hoover instructed FBI field offices to make "thorough, discreet and complete investigations" of 33 different political groups, including the American Youth Congress, the American Student Union, and the National Negro Congress.

J. Edgar Hoover served as the director of the Federal Bureau of Investigation (FBI) for almost half a century, during which time the agency was criticized for violating civil liberties. *(Library of Congress, Prints and Photographs Division, LC-USZ62-92411)*

THE JAPANESE INTERNMENT

The Japanese attacked Pearl Harbor, Hawaii, on December 7, 1941, bringing the United States into World War II. Japan staged this attack prior to publicly declaring war on the United States. The war years tested the nation's commitment to civil liberties. Japan's air attack and bombing of the U.S. naval base at Pearl Harbor sent shock waves through the American people. The Japanese air force sank or damaged 21 ships, destroyed 188 U.S. aircraft, and damaged another 159. The casualties were 2,403 military killed, 68 civilians killed, and 1,178 military and civilians wounded. President Roosevelt called the sneak attack a "day that will live in infamy." Overnight, Japanese Americans became suspects, and existing prejudices were inflamed.

"[An] emergency does not abrogate the Constitution or dissolve the Bill of Rights."

—*Attorney General Frank Murphy, 1942*

On February 17, 1942, Attorney General Francis Biddle reported to President Roosevelt that despite "increasing demands for evacuation of all Japanese, aliens and citizens alike, from the West Coast's states," and despite the fact that "many West Coast people distrust the Japanese" and would "welcome their removal from good farm land and the elimination of their competition," his most recent advice from the War Department and the FBI was that "there is no evidence of imminent attack" and "no evidence of planned sabotage."

Despite the lack of evidence, many people in the country feared that Japanese spies were active in the United States. With young men being sent overseas to fight and in light of Pearl Harbor, many

At Manzanar War Relocation Center in California, many of the 120,000 Japanese Americans were held throughout World War II, under Executive Order 9066, signed by President Franklin D. Roosevelt on February 19, 1942. *(Library of Congress, Prints and Photographs Division, LC-USZC4-5549)*

Americans wanted action they felt would make them safer. The president had promised that in the face of war, America would not "surrender the guarantees of liberty our forefathers framed for us in our Bill of Rights," but in 1942, FDR signed Executive Order 9066. This order authorized 120,000 residents in the United States of Japanese ancestry, two-thirds of whom were U.S. citizens, to be taken from their homes and offices and detained in camps where they were confined for the duration of the war.

Despite court challenges at the time to the internments from ACLU affiliates in California, the Supreme Court upheld the actions of the government. The justices who dissented from those decisions called the internment "a clear violation of constitutional rights," dropping the country into "the ugly abyss of racism."

Years later the courts would find that the U.S. government had violated the rights of assembly and association of Japanese Americans who were interned. In 1984, Fred Korematsu, an American citizen of Japanese ancestry whose 1942 conviction for violating the exclusion order had been upheld by the U.S. Supreme Court, won a reversal of his conviction. The U.S. District Court ruled that the government had deliberately provided misleading information to the Supreme Court to justify the threat to national security posed by Japanese-American civilians in the United States.

THE COLD WAR

World War II ended in 1945. However, the hot war against Germany, Italy, and Japan was replaced by what became known as the cold war with the Soviet Union. Although the Soviets were American allies during the war, disagreements began soon after. Germany—and its capital, Berlin—was split into sectors, each occupied by an Allied force. In 1948, the Soviets, who controlled the sector around Berlin, closed access to the French, British, and U.S. sectors in the western part of that city. The United States responded by airlifting in food and other vital supplies to the stranded residents of West Berlin for 11 months.

Such Soviet actions played a major role in creating the climate of suspicion that pervaded much of postwar America. In this highly charged cold-war atmosphere the FBI spied on people suspected of "Communist sympathies" often based on no evidence or such weak evidence as subscribing to a magazine or attending a meeting. If a

"If a person says that in this country Negroes are discriminated against and there is inequality of wealth, there is every reason to believe that person is a Communist."

—*Albert Canwell, chair of the Washington State Un-American Activities Committee, 1949*

non-Communist happened to agree with the Communists on a particular issue they were treated as if they were a Communist.

The FBI was responding to what it perceived as a serious threat to national security. Americans in every walk of life across the political spectrum were fearful that communism endangered the nation. People were worried about subversion and sabotage, by secret Communist cells controlled by the Soviet Union.

In this atmosphere people were reluctant to join any organization or attend any meeting that might get them in trouble, even if they were not doing anything illegal. The damage to freedom of association and freedom of assembly in such circumstances can be enormous. For fear of being accused of being disloyal, people steered clear of even the most innocent situations, such as going to a bookstore to listen to a reading or attending a meeting to hear a speaker, let alone joining an organization or speaking out on an important political issue.

Assessing the threat to national security posed by communism in postwar America is a complex undertaking. While it is safe to say, based on recent analysis of previously sealed Soviet and U.S. records, there were Communist spies helping the Russians who

"WITCH HUNTS"

With HUAC, FBI spying, and the Smith Act firmly in place, the period from the late 1940s to the mid-1960s prompted a "witch hunt" reminiscent of events in 1692 in Salem, Massachusetts. From June through September of that year, as hysteria and fear that the devil had taken possession of many townspeople, 19 men and women were convicted of witchcraft and hung at Gallows Hill. One man of over 80 years was pressed to death under heavy stones for refusing to submit to a trial on witchcraft charges. Hundreds of others faced accusations of witchcraft. Dozens languished in jail for months without trials. The term *witch hunt* has since referred to any period in which panic over a threat, real or imagined, leads to false accusations against people who are then harassed, humiliated, persecuted, and even convicted of crimes they never committed.

worked within the U.S. government, it is also safe to say that the FBI, its informants, and anti-Communist politicians exaggerated the extent and importance of the espionage. Nonetheless, because communism was perceived as such a grave threat, it took very little evidence to convince most Americans that every Communist was a spy. In that climate, even well-intentioned measures to protect national security could be abused and acts of political repression, which would never have been condoned under other circumstances, were tolerated by the public and a broad spectrum of political leaders and other decision makers.

Loyalty Oaths

On March 21, 1947, President Harry Truman signed Executive Order 9835 creating the Federal Loyalty Program, which allowed the government to deny employment to anyone if "reasonable grounds exist for belief that the person involved is disloyal to the Government of the United States." Evidence of disloyalty could include "membership in, affiliation with or sympathetic association with any foreign or domestic organization, Communist, or subversive, or as having adopted a policy of advocating or approving the commission of acts of force or violence to deny other persons their rights." Truman directed his attorney general to draw up an official list of "subversive" organizations.

Despite legitimate concerns over national security, the Loyalty Program posed a serious danger to freedom of assembly and freedom of association. Since the terms *subversive* and *sympathetic association* were undefined, a person could easily be labeled a "Communist sympathizer" just for supporting causes, such as racial equality or freedom of speech, which Communists also supported. Once on the list there was no procedure for an organization to challenge the "subversive" designation. And once the government discovered that anyone holding or applying for a federal job was a member of a listed organization, they could be fired or rejected without any hearing or chance to defend themselves.

On December 4, 1947, Attorney General Tom Clark, who would later be appointed to the U.S. Supreme Court, issued the first official list of subversive organizations. It contained 82 groups, including not only the Communist Party but also the National Negro Congress, the Joint Anti-Fascist Refugee Committee, and

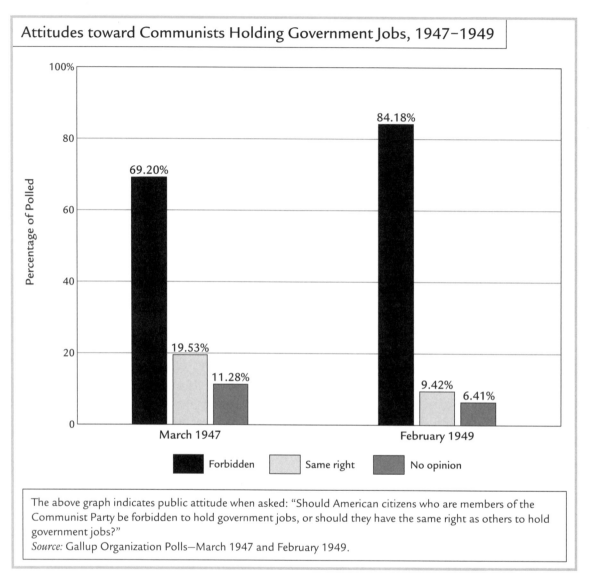

Attitudes toward Communists Holding Government Jobs, 1947–1949

The above graph indicates public attitude when asked: "Should American citizens who are members of the Communist Party be forbidden to hold government jobs, or should they have the same right as others to hold government jobs?"
Source: Gallup Organization Polls—March 1947 and February 1949.

Fear of communism ran high in America after World War II. Despite the fact that membership in the Communist Party was legal, large majorities believed that even American citizens who were members of the party should be forbidden from holding government jobs.

International Labor Defense. Although the list had been prepared only to deal with federal employees under the Loyalty Program, it quickly became a handy "blacklist" used by state and local governments. The term *blacklist* refers to any list of suspected persons who are excluded from a job or other benefit, usually under questionable circumstances, without having any opportunity to question why they are on the list in the first place.

On behalf of the Joint Anti-Fascist Refugee Committee (JAFRC), the ACLU argued to the Supreme Court that being on the list had caused the loss of tax-exempt status, denial of licenses to solicit funds, rejection of permits to hold public meetings, and a decline in memberships and contributions, thereby violating the members' freedom of assembly, association, and speech. A sharply divided Supreme Court issued six different opinions, but ruled on a narrow procedural point that JAFRC should not have been put on the list. The Court never ruled on the constitutionality of the list itself, which remained on the books until 1974.

THE HOLLYWOOD TEN

When several prominent motion picture writers, who became known as the Hollywood Ten, refused to name names at the HUAC hearings, they were each held in contempt of Congress and sent to jail for between six and 12 months. The writers were Herbert Biberman, Lester Cole, Albert Maltz, Adrian Scott, Samuel Ornitz, Dalton Trumbo, Edward Dmytryk, Ring Lardner, Jr., John Howard Lawson, and Alvah Bessie. The ACLU challenged their punishment, arguing that under the First Amendment, "no general inquiry into matters relating to opinion or affecting freedom of association is permissible." But all of the court challenges, which continued until 1958, failed. Eventually, more than 320 writers, actors, and performers were blacklisted from Hollywood and prevented from working on suspicion of being Communists, including Stella Adler, Leonard Bernstein, Charlie Chaplin, Aaron Copland, Dashiell Hammett, Lillian Hellman, Burl Ives, Arthur Miller, Dorothy Parker, Pete Seeger, Zero Mostel, Clifford Odets, John Randolph, Orson Welles, Paul Robeson, and Richard Wright. Some blacklisted screenwriters continued to write under assumed names. Two of these writers, Dalton Trumbo (*Roman Holiday* [1953] and *The Brave One* [1956]) and Michael Wilson (*Bridge Over the River Kwai* [1957]) won Academy Awards for their screenplays.

Robert Thompson (left) and Benjamin Davis (right), as they leave the Federal Courthouse in New York City, are surrounded by protesters demanding fair trials for Communists accused of violating the Smith Act. *(Library of Congress, Prints and Photographs Division, LC-USZ62-111434)*

In October 1947, HUAC opened hearings on the alleged "Communist influence" in the motion picture industry. Individuals were forced to appear before the committee, not only to admit whether they had ever been members of the Communist Party, but to name anyone else who had been. During World War II, the United States and the Soviet Union had been allies against Germany, and in the 1930s and 1940s many Americans had joined the Communist Party because it opposed Nazism, stood for racial equality, and supported the rights of workers to higher wages and better working conditions. With the war over and the cold war against the Soviet Union in progress, the political climate had changed, and past membership in the Communist Party was now considered "subversive" and grounds for public humiliation and worse.

Boosted by its success in court, HUAC continued to hold public hearings in Los Angeles; Detroit; Chicago; Philadelphia; Gary, Indiana; and San Francisco. Witnesses who invoked their constitutional right not to testify under the Fifth Amendment, which protects individuals from casting guilt upon themselves, were ridiculed as "Fifth Amendment Communists." Private organizations also got into the business of blacklisting in the 1950s, expanding from Hollywood to the radio and television industries. American Business Consultants published a list of 151 alleged subversives in its publication *Red Channels* and was paid by sponsors and broadcasters to "clear" employees, by proving that they were not Communists.

Meanwhile, the federal government continued to enforce the Smith Act against suspected Communists. In *Dennis v. United States,* the Supreme Court upheld the constitutionality of the law. In dissent, Justice Hugo Black warned that the majority of the Court was reducing the First Amendment to where it would protect only " 'safe' or orthodox views which rarely need its protection."

In this atmosphere, in 1949, 15 states enacted their own loyalty oaths for public employees. By 1951, 39 states had done so. Eventually, 42 states and more than 2,000 local jurisdictions required loyalty oaths for all public employees. Several loyalty oaths were challenged in Maryland, Pennsylvania, New York, Michigan, Illinois, and California by a wide array of organizations, including the Young Women's Christian Association (YWCA) and the American Association of University Professors (AAUP), as well as the ACLU and Americans for Democratic Action.

The oaths posed a particularly grave threat to what the AAUP perceived as freedom of association and academic freedom. In California by 1950, more than 300 professors had refused to sign loyalty oaths, including a full 20 percent of the faculty at the University of California at Berkeley. Although at first the U.S. Supreme Court upheld the loyalty oaths, eventually, in 1964, in the case of *Baggett v. Bullitt,* brought by the AAUP and the ACLU, the court struck them down.

A study of the loyalty oath program conducted by author and professor of history Ellen Schrecker concludes that the FBI's inflated assessment of the Communist threat and its politically conservative standards of evidence led to "widespread injustice," with

"I do solemnly swear (or affirm) that I will support the Constitution of the United States and the Constitution of the State of California, and that I will faithfully discharge the duties of my office according to the best of my ability; and that I am not a member of the Communist Party or under any oath or a party to any agreement or under any commitment that is in conflict with my obligations under this oath."

—*California loyalty oath, 1949*

thousands of government workers and hundreds, maybe thousands, of workers in the private sector losing their jobs.

In 1950, Congress passed the Internal Security Act, known as the McCarran Act, which required Communist and "Communist-action" organizations to register with the new Subversive Activities

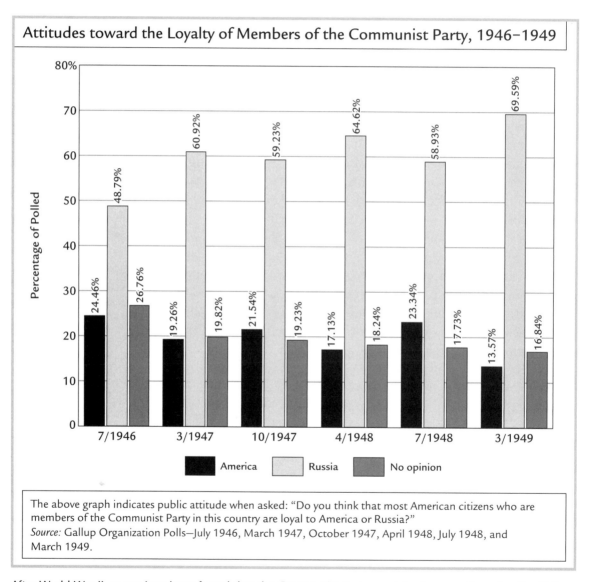

Attitudes toward the Loyalty of Members of the Communist Party, 1946–1949

The above graph indicates public attitude when asked: "Do you think that most American citizens who are members of the Communist Party in this country are loyal to America or Russia?"
Source: Gallup Organization Polls—July 1946, March 1947, October 1947, April 1948, July 1948, and March 1949.

After World War II, many Americans feared that the Communist Party was intent on overthrowing the U.S. government. Consequently, by 1949 almost 70 percent believed that most American citizens who were members of the Communist Party were loyal to Russia, not the United States.

Amid McCarthyism, some protesters worried more about the development of nuclear weapons. *(Library of Congress, Prints and Photographs Division, LC-USZ62-113632)*

Control Board (SACB) and to disclose their officers, finances, and membership lists. The consequences of being listed with SACB were severe, including denial of a passport and ineligibility for government employment.

McCarthyism

In February 1950, Joseph McCarthy, a U.S. senator from Wisconsin, made a speech in which he claimed to have a list of 57 people in the U.S. State Department known to be members of the American Communist Party. At this time, the United States was involved in the Korean War, which was not going well. Communists were making advances in Eastern Europe and in China, and the American public was frightened about the possibility that Communists could secretly infiltrate the United States and overthrow the government.

McCarthy was made chairman of the Senate Government Committee on Operations. For the next two years McCarthy's committee investigated various government departments and questioned scores of people about their political affiliations. Some lost their jobs after they admitted they had been members of the Communist Party. McCarthy made it clear to the witnesses that the only way to show that they had abandoned their left-wing views was to name other members of the party. The resultant witch hunt and anti-Communist hysteria became known as "McCarthyism."

At first, McCarthy targeted Democrats associated with President Roosevelt's New Deal policies of the 1930s that, by supporting the poor, the unemployed, and working people, were easily distorted to seem like "pro-Communist" programs. President Harry Truman and members of his Democratic administration were accused of being "soft" on communism, that is, too lenient and tolerant. With Truman being portrayed as a dangerous liberal, McCarthy's campaign helped the Republican candidate, Dwight Eisenhower, win the presidential election in 1952.

McCarthy's next target was what he called "anti-American" books in libraries. His staff looked into the Overseas Library Program and discovered 30,000 books they claimed were written by "communists, pro-communists, former communists and anti–anti-communists." After the publication of the list, the books were removed from library shelves to "protect" people from reading subversive material.

In October 1953, McCarthy began investigating Communist infiltration in the U.S. military. He attempted to discredit Robert Stevens, the secretary of the army. President Eisenhower was furious and realized that it was time to put an end to McCarthy's reckless activities.

The Tide Turns Against McCarthyism

On March 9, 1954, Edward R. Murrow, an experienced television broadcaster, used his popular program *See It Now* to condemn McCarthy's methods. Prominent newspaper columnists such as Walter Lippman and Jack Anderson became more open in their attacks on McCarthy.

The Senate investigations into the U.S. Army were televised, and this also helped to expose McCarthy's tactics. One newspaper, the *Louisville Courier-Journal,* reported: "In this long, degrading travesty of the democratic process McCarthy has shown himself to be evil and possessed of unmatched malice." Leading politicians in both parties had been embarrassed by McCarthy's performance and on December 2, 1954, a censure motion in the Senate condemned his conduct by 67 votes to 22.

McCarthy lost the chairmanship of his Senate committee. Without a power base and public platform, the media lost interest in his claims of a Communist conspiracy.

By the late 1950s, anticommunism began to subside and the public's tolerance for witch-hunting began to give way to greater concern for constitutional rights.

These changes were reflected in several Supreme Court decisions striking down cold-war measures. The Court unanimously held that an individual could not be denied admission to practice law based upon past membership in the Communist Party. A conviction for perjury was overturned because the defendant had not been allowed to examine FBI reports about an unidentified FBI informant on whose testimony the prosecution was based. The court limited the use of the Smith Act by distinguishing between actual *advocacy* of overthrowing the government and merely teaching such a course of action as an *abstract doctrine*. The Court also overturned a HUAC contempt conviction of a union official who willingly testified about his own association with the Communist Party but refused to "name names" of others. The Court stated that "there is no congressional power to expose for the sake of exposure."

The cloud over a dark chapter in American history was beginning to lift. For doing nothing more than exercising their constitutional rights, many people had been punished wrongfully. Freedom of assembly and association had suffered.

"Men who have in the past done effective work exposing Communists in this country have, by reckless talk and questionable methods, made themselves the issue rather than the cause they believe in so deeply."

—*Vice President Richard Nixon, March 4, 1954*

6

Wars in Vietnam and Iraq

The protests against the Vietnam War in the late 1960s and early 1970s involved massive demonstrations in Washington, D.C., New York City, and other major cities. Hundreds of thousands of protesters marched in the streets, carrying signs demanding that the United States withdraw from Vietnam. A march on Washington to protest the war in November 1969 attracted more than 500,000 demonstrators, making it the largest single protest in U.S. history and the largest exercise of freedom of assembly in America up to that point.

The impact was immense. As doubts about U.S. involvement in Vietnam grew, these large antiwar demonstrations, routinely broadcast on national television, suggested that the protesters represented even greater opposition within the general public than they actually did. These historic protests exemplified the collective power of assembly. The sheer number of protesters joining together magnified the effect of what any one of them individually could say.

THE FBI

As J. Edgar Hoover and the FBI had disrupted the civil rights movement, so, too, they disrupted opposition to the Vietnam War. Instead of seeing the antiwar movement as an expression of legitimate dissent protected by the Constitution, Hoover saw the protesters as potentially dangerous threats to the U.S. government and U.S. military operations.

To gain support from President Lyndon Johnson for his efforts to disrupt the antiwar movement, Hoover appealed to the last vestiges of anticommunism that still remained in American life. With little or no evidence, Hoover routinely reported to Johnson that there was Communist "influence" in the antiwar movement. By feeding on Johnson's fear of communism, Hoover strengthened the president's willingness to dismiss the antiwar movement as a small fringe effort, possibly orchestrated by foreign powers, which did not represent a growing opposition to the war.

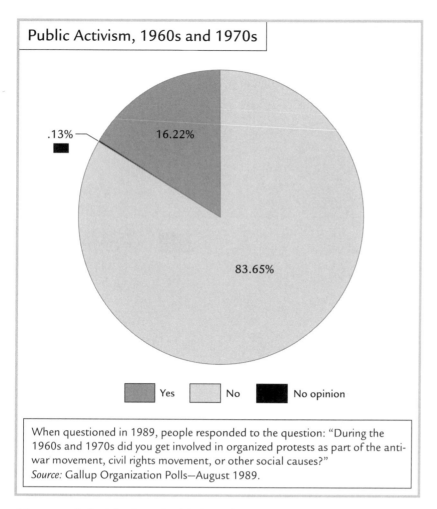

Public Activism, 1960s and 1970s

.13%

16.22%

83.65%

▮ Yes   ▯ No   ■ No opinion

When questioned in 1989, people responded to the question: "During the 1960s and 1970s did you get involved in organized protests as part of the anti-war movement, civil rights movement, or other social causes?"
Source: Gallup Organization Polls—August 1989.

Many people look back on the 1960s and 1970s as a period of political activism. But when asked about the period years later, only about 16 percent said they were personally involved in organized protest as part of the antiwar movement, civil rights movement, and other social causes.

Commenting on Johnson's assumption that the antiwar movement was Communist-inspired, a later Senate report considered it "impossible to measure the larger impact on the fortunes of the nation from this distorted perception at the very highest policy-making level."

Even though the majority of Americans supported the war in Vietnam in its early stages, there is no question that the antiwar movement generated widespread opposition to U.S. policy in Vietnam. There were at least 400 separate campus demonstrations against the war in the 1966–67 school year and 3,400 the following year. Despite some violent outbursts by students and incidents of police brutality and overreaction, by and large the demonstrations were peaceful. They generally involved groups of students, sometimes with the support of faculty and others, gathering in public locations on campus or in nearby towns or cities to march or rally

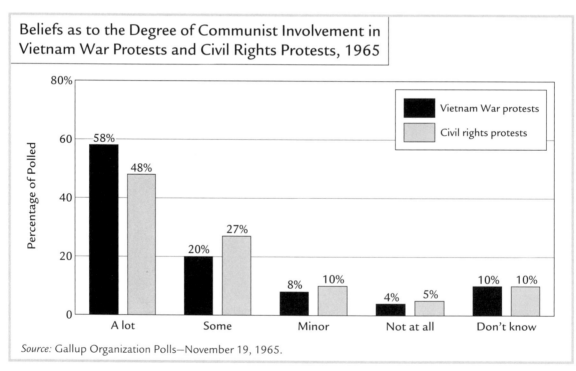

Beliefs as to the Degree of Communist Involvement in Vietnam War Protests and Civil Rights Protests, 1965

Source: Gallup Organization Polls—November 19, 1965.

Throughout the 1960s, a controversy raged over whether or not the antiwar and civil rights movements were under the influence of the Communist Party. In 1965, almost 90 percent of Americans believed there was Communist involvement in Vietnam War protests and almost 85 percent believed there was Communist involvement in civil rights protests.

carrying signs and chanting slogans expressing opposition to U.S. involvement in Vietnam.

The antiwar demonstrations represented a collective exercise of freedom of assembly. In some cases they involved only a dozen people, on other occasions hundreds and later thousands. The demonstrations showed the public that there were many who did not agree with government policy. Instead of people thinking they were alone in their opposition, the demonstrations revealed that there were many others who agreed.

While these public expressions of political opposition were occurring, fearing that the antiwar movement had been infiltrated by Communists and would breed disloyalty and resistance, the FBI attempted to disrupt them. Between 1968 and 1971, the FBI conducted 291 secret operations aimed at preventing individuals from antiwar groups from speaking out against the war, as well as creating false information ("disinformation") to confuse, demoralize, and disrupt antiwar organizations. Records were secretly being kept on thousands of individuals active in opposing the war. The FBI's first list was called the Rabble Rouser Index, followed by the Agitator Index and later the Key Activist Index. The FBI blocked dissidents from speaking, turned them against one another, and spread

KENT STATE

The election of Richard Nixon as president in 1968 increased war protests. Opponents of the war saw Nixon as a pro-war president who offered no realistic plan to get the United States out of Vietnam. When Nixon expanded the Vietnam War on April 30, 1970, by bombing neighboring Cambodia, campuses across the country erupted with massive protests. On May 4, National Guardsmen on the campus of Kent State University in Ohio fired into a crowd of students, killing four and wounding nine. To protest this brutal response, large demonstrations were held on 400 campuses in order to connect in the public imagination the deaths of the Kent State students to the deaths of civilians abroad. Hoover said that "the students invited and got what they deserved."

On November 15, 1969, a crowd of demonstrators, estimated at 200,000, gathers at the Washington Monument for the Moratorium Day peace rally to protest the Vietnam War. *(AP/Wide World Photos, 4839616)*

rumors to breed resentment, thereby blunting the effectiveness of the movement.

Ironically, one of the victims of Hoover's tactics was President Johnson himself. By failing to comprehend the depth of opposition to the war among mainstream Americans and by discounting the antiwar movement as a small, marginal group of disaffected students possibly under Communist influence, Johnson miscalculated the direction of the country and found himself headed to likely defeat if he ran for reelection. Johnson announced that he would not run in 1968.

J. Edgar Hoover died in 1972, and while Articles of Impeachment stemming from the Watergate scandal were pending in Congress, President Nixon resigned in 1974. The Vietnam War was over. The efforts of Hoover, the FBI, and two administrations to derail the antiwar movement had failed. The concerted effort of those opposed to U.S. involvement in Vietnam to voice their dissent through massive rallies, marches, and demonstrations had gained the attention of the media and the public. It forced average Americans generally inclined to support their government to question its policies and contributed significantly to ending the war.

This highly visible exercise of freedom of assembly had a profound impact on American history. Eventually millions of people concluded that if they joined with others to demonstrate their opposition, they could actually change what their government was doing—they could stop a war. No single protester believed he or she could do that alone, but all of the protesters believed they could do it together.

NEO-NAZIS IN SKOKIE

One of the greatest tests of freedom of assembly came in 1977 when a group of American neo-Nazis led by Frank Collins announced that they intended to march in Skokie, Illinois, a predominantly Jewish community, with the largest number of Holocaust survivors in the United States.

Collins, leader of a small group called the National Socialist Party of America (NSPA) that espoused racist views and opposed integration, announced that on May 1, 1977, he intended to stage a demonstration in front of the Skokie village hall. He expected about 50 demonstrators, some wearing neo-Nazi uniforms.

At first the mayor and village attorney granted the NSPA's request, but when Jewish groups learned of the prospect of Nazis marching in Skokie, they vehemently objected, prompting Skokie village officials to seek a court injunction banning Collins's demonstration. Collins contacted the ACLU, and the organization agreed to defend the group's constitutional rights.

The ACLU's decision would prove to be a turning point in the history of that organization and a major lesson in the history of freedom of assembly. It would test whether constitutional rights

THE ENVIRONMENTAL MOVEMENT

In 1892, legendary preservationist John Muir (1838–1914), who was born in Scotland and spent much of his life exploring the American wilderness, joined with several others who shared his love of nature to found the Sierra Club, the first group organized in America to protect and conserve the environment.

In 1905, the National Audubon Society was formed by various local and state Audubon groups whose main goal was to protect the nation's bird life. John James Audubon (1785–1851) had been a prominent artist known for his photolike paintings of birds and wildlife and so the society chose to use his name. The Audubon Clubs not only developed educational programs but also supported laws to prohibit the sale of bird plumes and restrict bird hunting. In doing so, these clubs were both exercising freedom of association and the right to petition the government for redress of grievance, by calling attention to the killing of birds for profit and sport.

In 1936, the first North American Wildlife Conference brought together representatives of the more than 35,000 preservationists clubs and groups that had been established all over the country. One of the principal speakers at the conference was J. N. Darling. He called on his fellow preservationists to take a path very few of them had pursued before: political action. He called on them to unify behind a clear set of goals and to achieve those goals by voting for candidates who spoke out for the preservationist platform. In response, they formed the General Wildlife Federation and elected Darling as its first president. In 1938, they changed their name to the National Wildlife Federation (NWF).

By actively petitioning the government for redress of grievances—in this case, protecting the environment—the NWF convinced Congress to pass a law imposing a tax on guns and using the money raised to support state wildlife protection programs. By the middle of the 20th century, what the preservationists and conservationists had

In the "Operation Breathe Free" motorcade in 1967, men, women, and children wear surgical masks before leaving South Beach, Staten Island, New York, to protest air pollution. *(Library of Congress, Prints and Photographs, LC-USZ62-121601)*

begun expanded into a much broader movement concerned not only with saving the pristine beauty of the wilderness but also with saving the Earth from pollution, overpopulation, and threats from nuclear war and nuclear power. Pollution results when dangerous chemicals, fertilizers, and weedkillers enter the water and air exposing people and animals to serious health problems and even death. Overpopulation is the risk that if too many people inhabit the Earth, there will not be enough food, water, and other resources to sustain them. Nuclear war is the threat that weapons using advanced nuclear science unleashed during war could kill millions of people and destroy entire nations. Nuclear power brings with it the possibility of accidents that might release radiation into the environment, as well as the problem of nuclear waste.

David Brower emerged as a movement leader. In 1952 Brower became the Sierra Club's first full-time, salaried director. He exhibited a keen skill for using letter-writing campaigns and newspaper ads to influence public opinion and elected officials to support environmental causes. With Brower at the helm, the Sierra Club grew from 7,000 members in 1952 to 77,000 in 1969. But disagreements within the organization forced him out, and he founded Friends of the Earth and later the League of Conservation Voters, which tracks the voting records of members of Congress on environmental legislation.

On April 22, 1970, the first Earth Day was held throughout the United States, to

Pollution from automobile exhaust fumes and industrial waste chokes the air and obscures the New York City skyline. *(Library of Congress, Prints and Photographs, LC-USZ62-114346)*

commemorate the importance of protecting the planet. The success of Earth Day reflected just how far the movement had come.

By exercising their freedom of assembly, freedom of association, and the right to petition the government for redress of grievances, in face of opposition from business interests and others who argued that such laws would retard progress and hurt the economy, activists in the environmental movement succeeded in getting the Clean Air Act (1955) and the Wilderness Preservation Act (1964) passed. In 1970 alone, Congress passed the

(continues)

(continued)

National Environmental Policy Act, the Occupational Safety and Health Act, the Solid Waste Disposal Act, and a stronger Clean Air Act.

For 12 years beginning in 1980, the administrations of Presidents Ronald Reagan and George H. W. Bush were more sympathetic to corporations and industries that opposed the environmental legislation that had been passed in the previous decade. The Reagan and Bush administrations reduced the budgets of the Environmental Protection Agency and abandoned programs to develop alternative energy sources, such as solar and wind power. Despite—or because of—resistance to environmental protection in the Reagan and Bush administrations, organizations dedicated to this cause continued to grow. By the end of the Reagan-Bush era, the Sierra Club had 580,000 members and 350 local groups; the Wilderness Society had 300,000 members; the National Wildlife Federation was sending its educational publication to more than 1 million children each month; and the National Audubon Society had 560,000 members in 512 local chapters.

The growth of the environmental movement is a dramatic example of the effective impact of freedom of assembly, freedom of association, and the right to petition the government for redress of grievances. By actively and creatively using these rights, environmentalists succeeded in changing the country. What no single person or small group could achieve, large groups and organizations have achieved. Pooling their time, money, ingenuity, and energy, members of these organizations were able to influence public opinion and, in turn, get laws passed to protect the environment and the health and lives of all Americans.

The country would be a far different place had preservationists, conservationists, and environmentalists not chosen to assemble, associate, and petition. The air, water, wildlife, and landscape of America would not be as clean, clear, safe, and preserved. By exercising these rights, environmentalists improved not only the lives of millions of Americans but also the world beyond. The protection and exercise of constitutional rights serve the interests of both the individuals involved and the wider community.

belong only to those who espouse acceptable views or also to those who stand for things that are hateful and contrary to the deepest-held views of a majority of Americans.

Skokie officials argued that the Nazis would incite a breach of the peace. The ACLU argued that under that theory the government could silence any group from exercising its rights of assembly and freedom of speech by merely speculating that disruptive behavior might ensue. At the trial-court level, Skokie won and the neo-Nazi march was stopped.

The Skokie government was not satisfied to just stop the march. The village passed three new laws: One required 30 days' advance notice of a protest and a $350,000 insurance policy; the next outlawed the public display of "symbols offensive to the community" and parades by political organizations wearing "military-style" uniforms; and the third banned the "dissemination of any material . . . which promotes and incites hatred against persons by reason of their race, national origin, or religion."

When the Illinois Supreme Court tried to avoid the ACLU's appeal of the injunction on a technicality, the U.S. Supreme Court stepped in and ruled that anyone who was being prevented in advance of exercising their constitutional rights, known as "prior restraint," was entitled to an immediate hearing.

SKOKIE AND THE ACLU

Though the Nazis eventually won the Skokie court battles, it may have been the ACLU that lost the most, at least in the short run. Outraged that the ACLU would defend neo-Nazis, reportedly 30,000 members quit the ACLU, triggering a financial disaster for the civil liberties group. In response, David Goldberger, a Jewish ACLU lawyer who had defended Collins, wrote a fund-raising letter on behalf of the ACLU. He calmly explained why the ACLU had taken the case as a matter of principle. He asked his readers to think what it would have meant if the government had prevailed. "Think of such power in the hands of a racist sheriff, or a local police department hostile to antiwar demonstrators, or the wrong kind of president." The Goldberger letter reminded people of just why it was imperative to protect the constitutional rights of those with whom they disagreed to ensure that the law would protect those with whom they agreed. In response, more than 25,000 people donated $550,000, making it the largest single fund-raising appeal in ACLU history. Today, the ACLU considers the Skokie case as an outstanding moment in its history. The organization stood up for principle, regardless of the popularity of its client.

When the Illinois Supreme Court addressed the case in late January 1978, it agreed with the ACLU and held that the injunction against the Nazi march and against the display of the swastika (the Nazi symbol) was unconstitutional. The next month a federal district court also found that the three new laws passed by Skokie were unconstitutional. The federal appellate court upheld that ruling and, by a 7-2 vote, the U.S. Supreme Court declined to intervene.

"BAN THE BOMB!"

For almost 100 years, people have organized throughout the United States (and around the world) to prevent war and the spread of dangerous weapons that threaten massive devastation. As early as 1917, the American Friends Service Committee (AFSC), part of the Quaker pacifist movement, called for disarmament. In 1945, when the United States dropped atomic bombs on Hiroshima and Nagasaki, Japan, a new era in warfare dawned. The development of nuclear energy in the 1950s brought with it the danger of nuclear radiation and nuclear accidents and waste.

To confront these dangers, leaders in the AFSC joined with Dr. Albert Schweitzer, Eleanor Roosevelt, Dr. Benjamin Spock, and others to form the Committee for a Sane Nuclear Policy (SANE) with the mission of developing "public support for a boldly conceived and executed policy which will lead mankind away from war and toward peace and justice." Calling on governments to "Ban the Bomb," SANE forged alliances with civil and human rights organizations and leaders, including Dr. Martin Luther King, Jr., and singer Harry Belafonte, as well as labor groups such as the International Association of Machinists. In the early 1960s, *Women*

Families march in 1962 outside the United Nations in a "ban the bomb" demonstration. *(Library of Congress, Prints and Photographs, LC-US762-126854)*

Strike for Peace rallied more than 100,000 women in 60 cities across America to protest atmospheric nuclear tests.

Through aggressive lobbying, public protests, and public education efforts,

Now that the Nazis had established the right to march in Skokie, they decided not to. Instead, on June 24, 1978, they held a brief 15-minute rally in downtown Chicago.

A NEW WAVE OF PROTESTS

Following the end of the Vietnam War, America saw few massive political demonstrations in the streets for almost 25 years. Every so

SANE achieved its first major victory in 1963 with the ratification of the Limited Nuclear Test Ban Treaty. In the 1970s, SANE's work was closely linked to the growing movement against the Vietnam War. In 1978, SANE led a successful fight against the development of MX mobile missiles in Utah and Nevada, thereby avoiding the risk of massive environmental damage.

In the 1980s, President Ronald Reagan pursued expanded development of nuclear weapons. In reaction, a grassroots-based organization known as the Nuclear Weapons Freeze Campaign (Freeze), was organized in St. Louis, Missouri, and Washington, D.C., to "freeze and reverse the nuclear arms race." In 1982, Freeze, working with local activists, placed initiatives on the ballot in towns and cities across the country. These efforts were largely symbolic, but they channeled grassroots energy into highly visible expressions of support for nuclear disarmament. Soon well-known elected officials including Senator Ted Kennedy and Representative (Mass.) Patricia Schroeder joined the fight and introduced legislation in Congress to reduce nuclear weapons.

In 1987, SANE and Freeze merged into SANE/FREEZE and in 1993, became Peace

Action, which has since broadened its mission to include the elimination of trading in conventional weapons and support for budgets that fund human, rather than military, needs. By 2004, Peace Action had attracted 85,000 members and succeeded on such issues as land-mine legislation, the Comprehensive Test Ban Treaty, the Nuclear Nonproliferation Treaty, a weapons trade Code of Conduct, and cuts in military spending.

In addition to national and international disarmament organizations, thousands of local antinuclear groups have emerged, often associated with colleges and universities. In 1988, one researcher counted some 8,000 separate organizations. In reviewing writer Lawrence S. Wittner's groundbreaking history of nuclear disarmament, Steve Breyman, director of the graduate program in science and technology studies at Rensselaer Polytechnic Institute, in Troy, New York, concluded that "[i]t has not been the wisdom, vision, or rationality of our leaders that has so far saved us from nuclear holocaust. Instead, it has been the determined efforts of millions of ordinary and not-so-ordinary organized citizens across the globe and across the decades that forced restraint upon reckless leaders."

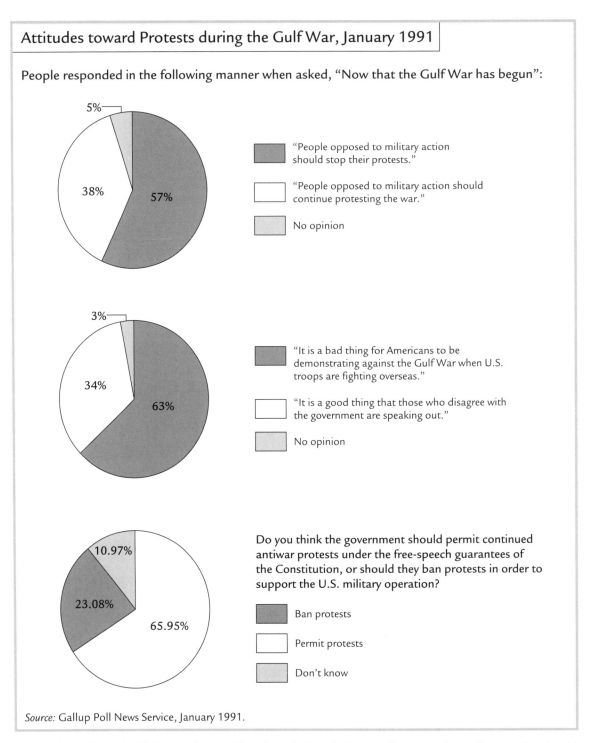

Attitudes toward Protests during the Gulf War, January 1991

People responded in the following manner when asked, "Now that the Gulf War has begun":

5%
38%
57%

"People opposed to military action should stop their protests."

"People opposed to military action should continue protesting the war."

No opinion

3%
34%
63%

"It is a bad thing for Americans to be demonstrating against the Gulf War when U.S. troops are fighting overseas."

"It is a good thing that those who disagree with the government are speaking out."

No opinion

10.97%
23.08%
65.95%

Do you think the government should permit continued antiwar protests under the free-speech guarantees of the Constitution, or should they ban protests in order to support the U.S. military operation?

Ban protests

Permit protests

Don't know

Source: Gallup Poll News Service, January 1991.

During the Gulf War in 1991, a majority of Americans believed that people opposed to military action should stop their antiwar protests, but when those polled were reminded of the guarantees of free speech in the Constitution, support for the right to protest reached almost two-thirds.

often certain political issues would spark sporadic protests but not on the scale of the marches and rallies during the 1960s and 1970s.

Pro-choice/Pro-life Groups and Assembly

The U.S. Supreme Court decision in *Roe v. Wade* in 1973 guaranteeing women the constitutional right to abortion ushered in a period of highly visible and sometimes violent antiabortion protests across the country. Pro-life activists with deeply held religious and moral objections to abortion began holding demonstrations outside abortion clinics, chanting slogans and holding up graphic photographs of aborted fetuses. In some cases, pro-life advocates blocked the entrances of the clinics, preventing women from getting inside.

The National Abortion Federation reports that between 1977 and 2004, there were 700 blockades of abortion clinics resulting in 33,830 arrests, with most of these blockades occurring between 1977 and 1994 (634 blockades, 33,661 arrests); between 1995 and 2004, there were only 66 blockades and 169 arrests.

In 1986, a group of men, including Randall Terry, founded Operation Rescue, which its supporters consider the largest social movement involving civil disobedience in American history. During those early years, thousands of men and women sat in front of abortion clinics to prevent what they called "the killing of innocent children" and paid the penalty in arrest and prosecution on trespassing charges.

Many Operation Rescue organizations cropped up across the country, including Operation Rescue of Los Angeles and Operation Rescue of San Diego. The California Operation Rescue organizations merged into one group, Operation Rescue of California, which was disbanded after an $880,000 judgment was won against them by Planned Parenthood in 1994.

The U.S. Supreme Court has been asked on several occasions to decide the limits of lawful antiabortion protests. In *Frisby v. Schultz* (1988), the Court upheld a ban on picketing on the sidewalk outside the personal residence of a doctor who performed abortions. In *Schenk v. Pro-Choice Network* (1997), the Court found a law that prevented protesters from coming within a 15-foot "floating buffer zone" surrounding a clinic patient violated the First Amendment. And in *Hill v. Colorado* (2000), the Court upheld a state statute that prohibited protesters within 100 feet of the entrance to any health-care facility from approaching within eight feet of another person, without that person's consent, for the purpose of passing out a leaflet, displaying a sign, or engaging in oral protest, education, or counseling.

In 1994, Congress enacted the Freedom of Access to Clinic Entrance (FACE) Act forbidding the use of "force, threat of force or physical obstruction" to prevent someone from providing or receiving reproductive health services. In several legal challenges, the constitutionality of FACE has been upheld. In one ruling, *American Life League, Inc. v. Reno* (1995), the U.S. Court of Appeals for the Fourth Circuit held that FACE does not violate the First Amendment, specifically stating that FACE "does not prohibit protestors from praying, chanting, counseling, carrying signs, distributing handbills or otherwise expressing opposition to abortion, so long as these activities are carried out in a non-violent, non-obstructive manner."

In 1998, a jury found that pro-life protesters had committed 121 crimes involving violent acts and threats of physical violence toward clinic staff and patients and awarded $257,780 in damages under the Racketeering Influenced and Corrupt Organizations Act (RICO). The trial court issued a permanent nationwide injunction prohibiting antiabortion organizations from obstructing access to abortion clinics, trespassing on clinic property, damaging clinic property, or using violence or the threat of violence against clinics, their employees, or their patients. But in 2003, the U.S. Supreme Court by an 8-1 vote in *Scheidler v. National Organization for Women* found that even though the defendants had interfered with the clinics, there was no evidence of the crime of "extortion," which was a prerequisite under RICO.

As the national debate over abortion continues, the question of where to draw the line between lawful and unlawful protest will continue to engage the attention of state and federal legislatures, the courts, and the public at large.

Direct Action

Frustrated by their failure to achieve their goals or motivated by ideological beliefs that attempt to justify the use of force to topple those in power, some social and political groups have rejected peaceful protest in favor of the use of violence.

In October 1969, members of Students for a Democratic Society (SDS) broke away to form the more radical Revolutionary Youth Movement, and they launched the so-called Days of Rage in Chicago, where they blew up a statue dedicated to police casualties killed in the 1886 Haymarket Riot. They rampaged through the city's business district, smashing windows and cars, resulting in six people being shot and 70 arrested.

The following year, the group adopted the name Weather Underground and called themselves Weathermen, based on the lyric of folksinger Bob Dylan, "You don't need a weatherman to know which way the wind blows." For the next six years, the loosely organized group issued a series of public statements advocating the overthrow of the government and condemning capitalism. The Weather Underground also conducted a series of bombings against the U.S. Capitol, the Pentagon, and police and prison buildings, generally preceded by telephone warnings to evacuate the sites to avoid loss of life. Members of the Weather Underground themselves were killed in an accidental explosion while they were preparing a bomb in a Greenwich Village apartment. Despite one of the largest FBI manhunts in history, the *Weathermen* avoided arrest. Some later came forward, and others melded into society pursuing careers in education and other fields.

The animal rights movement, seeking more humane treatment of animals used in medical experiments and commercial testing, also experienced a wave of violent episodes throughout its history. People for the Ethical Treatment of Animals (PETA), founded in 1980, is an international nonprofit organization based in Norfolk, Virginia, and committed to the principle that "animals are not ours to eat, wear, experiment on, or use for entertainment." PETA uses educational programs, boycotts, and highly visible demonstrations to draw attention to animal abuse and to promote the respectful treatment of animals. Other groups have gone much further. In testimony before a congressional hearing in 2002, an FBI spokesman claimed that radical groups such as the Earth Liberation Front (ELF) and the Animal Liberation Front (ALF) have engaged in over 600 criminal acts, causing over $43 million in damages and making them "the most dangerous domestic terrorist threat to the country." Working without any formal organization since the 1970s, ELF and ALF have claimed responsibility for thousands of acts of violence—including arson, destruction of equipment, release and stealing of animals, shooting at fishing boats, and even attempted murder—leading to numerous arrests and convictions all in the name of protecting the environment and animal rights. In 1999, another group, calling itself the "Justice Department," sent letters booby-trapped with razor blades to medical researchers and fur farms in the United States and Canada. Officially, PETA does not condone acts of violence and has not been implicated in the crimes attributed to ELF, ALF, or other radical groups. But critics claim that PETA rationalizes and celebrates such acts, and it has been accused of contributing money to such groups.

More recently, an animal rights organization originally organized in England has gained widespread notoriety in the United States. Stop Huntingdon Animal Cruelty (SHAC) has targeted Huntingdon Life Sciences, one of the largest animal testing companies in the world, because it has used primates, dogs, rabbits, pigs, and other animals for research to test chemicals, drugs, and cosmetics. In 2001, SHAC members beat the company's president with clubs outside his home in the United Kingdom. He survived, and one attacker served three years in jail for the incident.

SHAC also vandalized the homes of employees of Huntingdon's accounting firm and a pharmaceutical company that was a client of Huntingdon. SHAC claims responsibility for causing 87 businesses to end their relationship with Huntingdon. In May 2004, federal authorities in New Jersey, New York, California, and Washington state arrested seven members of SHAC on charges of conspiring to commit "animal enterprise terrorism," punishable by three years in prison. Prosecutors claimed that in most cases the individuals did not commit the actual crimes but posted inflammatory information on the Internet such as personal data about a target, who was eventually attacked, including addresses and children's names. Lawyers for the defendants claimed that the prosecution raised serious First Amendment issues, especially since officials sought to limit the defendants' online activity while awaiting trial. A spokeswoman for PETA questioned the government's motives in the SHAC arrests and asked whether "the right of freedom of association and free expression is now being stripped away in this country."

In another case that tested the bounds of freedom of assembly, four Christian protesters who were charged in July 2004 with criminal trespass for failing to leave the corporate headquarters of Alliant Tech Systems in Edina, Minnesota, where they were trying to deliver a letter and documents arguing that employees who manufacture weapons can be prosecuted under international law, were found not guilty after a jury trial. Under the defense of "a claim of right," the defendants successfully argued that it was reasonable for them to be on the property given the existence of international treaties to which the United States is bound. The defendants testified that they went to Alliant's offices to protest the manufacture of antipersonnel land mines, cluster bombs, and depleted uranium weapons that kill indiscriminately and therefore violate international law.

Since the 1970s there has also been a resurgence of the anarchist movement, which has appeared from time to time throughout American history. Anarchism is a political ideology that imagines a society without government in which individuals enjoy the utmost liberty. Some anarchists, known as "primitivists," go further and claim that civilization—not merely the state—needs to be abolished to truly foster liberty and a just social order. (Anarchy can also refer to a lawless and chaotic political situation, where all societal structures and institutions have broken down.)

Given that some anarchists historically have engaged in violent tactics including assassinations, such as the fatal shooting of President William McKinley in 1901, in recent times police officials and the media have sometimes assumed that all anarchists are dangerous and violent. Since the 1970s, a "punk" image of irresponsible youths has also been associated with the anarchist movement. The use of assassination and terrorism is condemned by most anarchists, but there are some who view violence as a form of "self-defense" and others who justify violent acts as a revolutionary means to provoke social upheaval, thereby transforming society for the good of the people. Other anarchists, some of whom trace their roots to Christian pacifism (the opposition to all wars), advocate that nonviolent resistance is the only method of achieving a truly anarchist revolution. They see violence as the basis of any government and argue that, as such, violence is illegitimate, no matter who is the target or the perpetrator.

The public's perception of anarchists is often fueled by the popular media. On the eve of the 2004 Republican National Convention, the *New York Daily News,* under the headline "Police Intelligence Warning: Anarchy Inc.," reported that "[p]olice believe 50 of the country's leading anarchists will be in the city for the convention." Most journalists and others who witnessed the massive demonstrations surrounding the RNC reported little or no violence from anarchists or other protesters.

Antiglobalization Groups and Assembly

In November 1999, large demonstrations were held in Seattle, Washington, protesting a conference of the World Trade Organization (WTO). Police and protesters clashed leading to many arrests, significant property damage, and subsequent lawsuits challenging the actions of the authorities.

The WTO conference was attended by foreign and trade ministers from 135 countries. Between 30,000 and 50,000 protesters arrived voicing environmental, labor, religious, and human rights objections to WTO policies.

Protest organizers had been making plans for several months through a loose coalition of community organizations called the Direct Action Network (DAN). DAN participants agreed to refrain from violence, physical or verbal; to not carry weapons; to not bring or use illegal drugs or alcohol; and to not destroy property. In advance of the demonstrations, leaders of DAN met with Seattle police and agreed upon a "script" in which protesters would engage in massive nonviolent civil disobedience and would be arrested en masse. By all accounts the events did not play out according to the "script," although reports differ on whether it was the police or the protesters that first used violent tactics.

When thousands of demonstrators blocked intersections as part of the nonviolent civil disobedience, the police did not arrest them as planned; instead, the crowds grew in size. Several eyewitness accounts corroborated by a police video indicate that shortly after 9:00 A.M. on the first day of protests, police in full body armor and accompanied by an armored personnel carrier began pushing nonviolent demonstrators and spraying them with pepper spray, followed by smoke and concussion grenades and volleys of rubber bullets and bean bags shot by the police.

Treating the police actions as an excuse to no longer remain nonviolent, about 30 individuals dressed in black proceeded to break windows at retail businesses and overturn newspaper racks.

Meanwhile, the right of the WTO delegates to attend their conference was seriously disrupted as they found themselves trapped in their hotels—city officials had not established cordoned-off routes for them to enter the conference facility.

At this point, a contingent of about 25,000 union members from 25 states, 50 unions, and 144 countries who had gathered for a rally at Memorial Stadium arrived in downtown Seattle as part of a march for which organizers had obtained a lawful permit. Later that afternoon the mayor of Seattle declared a state of emergency, prompting the governor of Washington to send in 200 National Guard troops and 300 state patrol officers. The next day, the mayor declared a 25-block area a "no protest zone" in which all expressions of political protest against the WTO were banned.

During the three days of protests a number of individuals, estimated between 25 and 200, spray-painted graffiti on downtown buildings, broke windows, threw objects at police, and broke into several retail stores including Nike, The Gap, and Starbucks. Some demonstrators, maintaining the pledge of nonviolence, tried to prevent the disruptive protesters from damaging property.

Early reports estimated property damage at $2.5 million. Subsequently downtown businesses estimated that they lost $20 million in pre-Christmas sales.

Authorities reported 148 injuries, including 92 civilians and 56 police officers, most of whom complained about inhalation of chemicals and hearing impairment from concussion grenades and other sonic deterrents. Observers estimated that more protesters may have been injured but did not go to the hospital for fear of being arrested.

According to the Seattle Police Department, out of 631 arrests, no charges were filed against 138. Of the 541 who were charged with misdemeanors, such as failure to disperse and obstructing pedestrians, charges were dropped against 373. Of the 24 misdemeanor cases that went to court, two were found guilty, 10 pleaded guilty, and two were acquitted. A total of 25 individuals were charged with felonies.

Within a week after the WTO protests ended, Seattle Police Chief Norm Stamper resigned, taking full responsibility for the disruption of the WTO and the ensuing chaos in the streets. He admitted that he knew in advance that the demonstrations were going to be very large and that he failed to provide sufficient support and backup for his officers. Seattle police and law enforcement officials outside the department, including the county sheriff, complained that the chief of police and city authorities were not prepared to handle the thousands of protesters who descended on the city for the WTO meeting.

In July 2000, the ACLU affiliate in Washington issued a 74-page report, "Out of Control: Seattle's Flawed Response to Protests Against the World Trade Organization," which concluded that "[c]ivil liberties paid a dear price for poor judgment calls made by public officials and police personnel every step of the way. The City must acknowledge what went wrong and take action to avoid similar mistakes in the future."

As a result, the city of Seattle was shut down during the protests, and a couple of city blocks were destroyed.

A NEW WAVE OF PROTESTS

The WTO protests ushered in a new wave of massive demonstrations that would eventually exceed those seen during the Vietnam War. Once again America's commitment to freedom of assembly and freedom of association would be tested at the 2000 national political conventions, during the build up to the war with Iraq, and again at the 2004 national political conventions. With the country divided over war and peace, the exercise of constitutional rights would test the resilience of the American system.

In summer 2000, the Republican Party held its national convention in Philadelphia, and the Democratic Party held its national convention in Los Angeles. In both cities, with the experience of the WTO in Seattle fresh in the minds of local officials and police, precautions were taken to control the demonstrators and prevent violence. The protesters wanted to stage highly visible events, which convention delegates and the media would be forced to observe. But the police and local authorities wanted to confine the protesters to remote "Free Speech Zones."

Both conventions experienced clashes between these competing interests, resulting in several injuries and arrests. In Los Angeles, the local ACLU affiliate challenged the Free Speech Zones in court and won an injunction requiring authorities to allow pro-testers to congregate just outside the convention hall where they could be seen and heard by the delegates and the news media.

Outside the Democratic National Convention, which was nom-inating Al Gore for president, the Los Angeles Police Department moved against thousands of protesters during a performance by the rock band Rage Against the Machine. The police reported that a few protesters had thrown stones, but organizers of the rally accused the police of overreacting and causing a riot. Journalists, legal observers, and protesters were injured in the ensuing melee as police on horseback charged into the crowd firing rubber bullets.

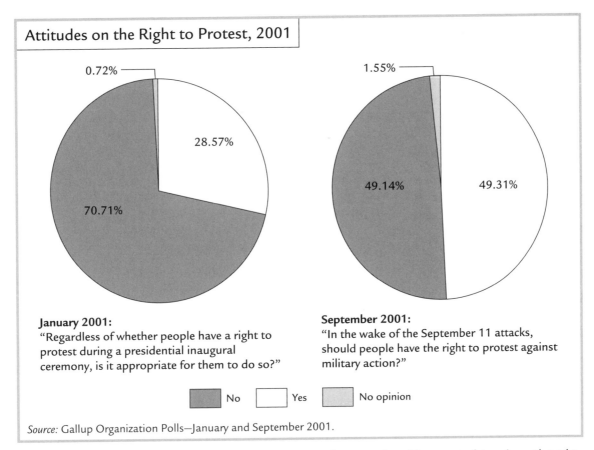

Attitudes on the Right to Protest, 2001

0.72%

28.57%

70.71%

1.55%

49.14%   49.31%

January 2001:
"Regardless of whether people have a right to protest during a presidential inaugural ceremony, is it appropriate for them to do so?"

September 2001:
"In the wake of the September 11 attacks, should people have the right to protest against military action?"

No   Yes   No opinion

Source: Gallup Organization Polls—January and September 2001.

In January 2001 when President George W. Bush was sworn in, more than 70 percent of Americans thought it was inappropriate to protest during the inaugural ceremony. Nine months later, after the terrorist attacks on September 11, Americans were equally divided over the right of people to protest against the United States taking military action.

After the 2000 Democratic National Convention, several lawsuits were eventually settled, with individuals who had been injured receiving monetary compensation from the City of Los Angeles.

That election season, George W. Bush became president in 2000. A year later, the country was attacked on September 11, 2001, catapulting the United States and much of the world into what Bush declared a "War on Terror." The country soon became sharply divided over how the United States should respond to the terrorist attacks. In that divisive political climate, opponents of the Bush administration used every means available to express their opposition and convince their fellow Americans to join them.

Shortly after September 11, peace groups and opponents of the Bush administration's foreign policy urged the United States to respond to terrorism by upholding the rule of law through the United Nations. Instead, the United States and some of its allies invaded Afghanistan and overthrew the Taliban regime, which had been accused of harboring terrorists including Osama bin Laden, the head of al-Qaeda whom the United States had accused of masterminding the September 11 attacks.

The USA PATRIOT Act

During the war in Afghanistan, at home, the Bush administration proposed the USA PATRIOT (Uniting and Strengthening America by Providing Appropriate Tools Required to Intercept and Obstruct Terrorism) Act within weeks after September 11. Despite serious concerns over potential civil liberties violations, the PATRIOT Act swept through Congress and was signed into law on October 26, 2001. The act contained several provisions that many observers feared would violate constitutional rights, including freedom of assembly, freedom of association, and the right to petition the government for redress of grievances.

For example, the PATRIOT Act created a new crime of "domestic terrorism," defined as anyone who breaks the law, in a way that is considered dangerous to human life for the purpose of intimidating or coercing a change in government policy. Critics of the PATRIOT Act pointed out that under this definition, if a group of antiwar activists engaged in peaceful, nonviolent civil disobedience by, for example, blocking the Golden Gate Bridge in San Francisco to protest the war in Afghanistan, they could be prosecuted for "domestic terrorism." They had indeed broken the law, they intended to intimidate or coerce a change in government policy, and a prosecutor could convince a jury that the protest was "dangerous to human life" by, for example, preventing ambulances or fire trucks from crossing the bridge or by distracting motorists. Consequently, an act of peaceful civil disobedience that would in the past be punished as a misdemeanor with a few days in jail and a nominal fine could now be transformed into a felony under the PATRIOT Act, with years in jail and a substantial fine.

The adverse impact on freedom of assembly and freedom of association of the "domestic terrorism" provision could be considerable. By increasing criminal punishments for peaceful, nonviolent conduct, individuals might be less inclined to join lawful but controversial organizations or participate in such activities.

Another provision of the PATRIOT Act that presented similar issues made it a crime to provide "material support" to any "terrorist organization." On its face, few could object to punishing someone who gives weapons or financial support to an organization whose avowed purpose is to terrorize and kill innocent people. Yet in January 2004, a U.S. district court in Los Angeles struck down the "material support" provision of the PATRIOT Act because it was so vague and ambiguous that a lawyer defending an organization labeled as "terrorist" could be charged with violating the PATRIOT Act.

A law that can be applied in this fashion could prompt people to steer clear of its provisions, thereby tending to discourage them from joining or supporting organizations that could be entirely innocent of any terrorist activities. Vague and uncertain laws that affect constitutional rights have been struck down by the courts because such laws fail to create a bright line distinguishing between what is legal and what is illegal.

War Against Iraq

In 2002, the Bush administration announced that it was prepared to invade the country of Iraq on the grounds that it had weapons of mass destruction (WMDs), which it intended to launch against the United States and its allies; that Iraq supported the terrorists who attacked the United States on September 11; and that Saddam Hussein, the leader of Iraq, was an evil dictator who should be removed so that the Iraqi people could enjoy freedom and democ-

> "As Americans we have to let our president know if we disagree with his plans to go to war."
>
> —*Terry Lewis, a protester from Virginia, 2003*

racy. At that point, international weapons inspection teams, led by Hans Blix and Mohamed El Baradei, were still searching for WMDs in Iraq. Iraq denied having any WMDs and granted access to its facilities for the inspections.

The question of whether or not to invade Iraq propelled America into the most sustained, outspoken, and divisive debate since the Vietnam War. The stakes were high. Should Americans be sent to Iraq to risk life and limb to depose Saddam Hussein before the weapons inspectors completed their work? Bush resoundingly told the country and the world that they should. His opponents were equally convinced that they should not.

The demonstrations at the WTO in Seattle in 1999 and at the national party conventions in 2000 looked like mere rehearsals for the massive protests that would be mounted in opposition to Bush's claims to invade Iraq. In January 2003, large peace rallies were held in Washington, D.C., and San Francisco, each attracting tens of thousands of protesters. Organizers said they had arranged for transportation from more than 200 cities in 45 states and estimated that about 200,000 participated in Washington, D.C., alone. The demonstrations in the United States were reinforced by peace rallies in 25 countries around the world.

The largest number of antiwar demonstrations in the history of the United States took place on February 15, 2003, with protests in 150 different cities, involving hundreds of thousands of people in many states. Organizers estimated the crowd in New York City at more than 375,000, but the police placed the turnout at 100,000. The main demonstration stretched 20 blocks down First Avenue. Police reported 50 arrests. A CNN producer reported seeing police use pepper spray on demonstrators.

The protests in the United States were matched by more than 600 antiwar rallies around the world. More than 3 million people marched in Rome, between 1 and 2 million in London, more than 600,000 in Madrid, and 300,000 in Berlin. By all accounts, this was the largest single day of protest in world history.

Hundreds of thousands of people had peaceably assembled across the nation to express their deeply held opposition to government policy. At no time in American history have so many people come together on a single day to voice their dissent. At no time in American history has the right to assemble been exercised on such a massive scale.

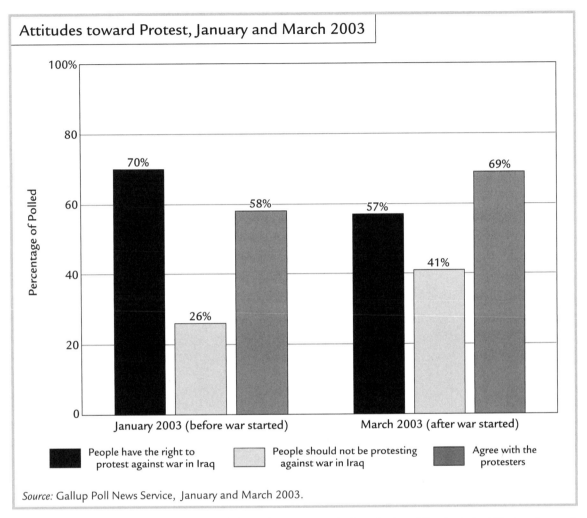

Attitudes toward Protest, January and March 2003

Source: Gallup Poll News Service, January and March 2003.

While a vast majority of people supported the right to protest before the Iraq War started, attitudes changed once hostilities began. On the other hand, faced with the realities of war, agreement with the antiwar protesters grew significantly.

In New York, approximately 1,000 demonstrators also voiced support for President Bush. In Wausau, Wisconsin, about 200 war supporters repeatedly interrupted antiwar speakers with chants of "George Bush, free Iraq" or "U.S.A., U.S.A."

On March 19, 2003, President Bush launched an invasion of Iraq with 250,000 U.S. troops and about 48,000 troops from three other nations. On May 1, 2003, Bush announced an end to major combat operations, but the war in Iraq continued. Saddam Hussein was captured on December 13, 2003, but no weapons of mass destruction were found. By late July 2005, more than 1,780 U.S. troops had been killed, and more than 180 soldiers from coalition forces had died. Reports of Iraqi casualties varied widely—from 5,000 to 124,000 soldiers and from 13,000 to 41,000 civilians.

Republican National Convention

In August 2004, the Republican Party held its national convention in New York City to renominate Bush to run for a second term. A month earlier, the Democratic Party held its convention in Boston, Massachusetts, and nominated Senator John Kerry to run for president. Given that Bush was the incumbent, it was anticipated that the protests at the Republican National Convention (RNC) would be highly visible and vocal.

For months, protesters sought permission from New York City to hold a huge demonstration with sound amplification on the Great Lawn in Central Park. United for Peace and Justice (UPJ), a coalition of more than 80 different organizations, led the fight. The city denied the permit, arguing that the expected 250,000 protesters would ruin the lawn, which the city had spent $18 million reseeding. When UPJ went to court, a state court judge sided with the city. One protester complained that it was "the rights of free speech versus the rights of lawn care, and the wrong side won." A separate lawsuit in federal court filed by the National Council of Arab Americans and the ANSWER [Act Now to Stop War and End Racism] Coalition, seeking permission for a separate demonstration in Central Park on the anniversary of the 1963 March on Washington, was also denied.

The setbacks in court hardly dampened the protesters' will to protest. On Friday, August 27, 2004, a vigil was held during which 972 pairs of military boots were displayed to represent the number of American deaths in the war in Iraq to that date. Meanwhile 5,000 protesters on bicycles rode through the streets of New York chanting slogans against Bush.

On Saturday, August 28, 2004, 25,000 pro-choice protesters marched in New York. The event, the largest pro-choice march in 30 years, was entirely peaceful, and there were no arrests.

That changed in succeeding days. On Sunday, August 29, 2004, the day before the RNC opened, an estimated 250,000 protesters

Thousands of demonstrators, organized by United for Peace and Justice, fill the streets of Manhattan on August 29, 2004, to protest the Republican National Convention. *(AP/Wide World Photos, 7436351)*

marched past Madison Square Garden, where the convention was being held. It was the largest demonstration at a political convention in U.S. history. The marchers included the young and old, people of all races, and people of various political persuasions. Some of them were members of UPJ, Planned Parenthood, the War Resisters League, Code Pink (a women's antiwar group), AFL-CIO, Act Up, and the National Lawyers Guild. Some marchers were not affiliated with any organizations.

The protests continued throughout the RNC, which ended on Thursday, September 2, 2004. By and large the protesters were

---

CONTROVERSY OVER POLICE ACTIONS AT RNC PROTESTS

The New York Civil Liberties Union (NYCLU) released a preliminary report shortly after the 2004 Republican National Convention ended complaining about the actions of the New York Police Department: "The pre-emptive arrests; preventative detentions and dangerous conditions at Pier 57 and massive surveillance of lawful protest activity undermined the right to dissent. Nonetheless, hundreds of thousands of people were demonstrating on the streets and sidewalks of New York throughout the course of the week," said Donna Lieberman, executive director of the NYCLU. The NYCLU questioned several actions by the NYPD, including preemptive arrests on the heels of a negotiated agreement on the terms for a lawful march; indiscriminate arrests of the press, legal observers, medics, and passersby; dangerous tactics such as the police suddenly charging into the crowd with metal barricades, a squad of plainclothes officers driving scooters into the crowd, and kicking, punching, or hitting with batons by police, as reported by some arrestees and bystanders; dangerous conditions at the Pier 57 detention facility, including detaining arrestees in a dank, filthy bus depot where they had to sit or lie on a floor covered with soot and what may have been toxic automotive fluids; excessive delays in processing arrestees of 36 hours or more on minor offenses; and pervasive police surveillance including videotaping and use of surveillance cameras to record lawful protest activity.

peaceful, and there was no property damage. But when it was over, it was reported there had been 1,821 arrests. Controversy swirled around some of the tactics used by the police.

According to the New York Civil Liberties Union (NYCLU), the police generally did a good job protecting protest at the permitted events so that hundreds of thousands of people were allowed to demonstrate loudly and peacefully around the RNC. At some of the spontaneous or nonpermitted demonstrations, the police responded with flexibility and cooperation. However, the NYCLU complained that there were "far too many problems, particularly at the non-permitted events when the police swooped in and illegally arrested hundreds of law abiding protestors."

As of May 2005, according to the Manhattan district attorney's office, of the 1,610 that had been resolved, 10 percent were convicted or pleaded guilty to misdemeanors, 26 percent were acquitted or dismissed, and the rest were postponed in contemplation of dismissal, with the files sealed if the defendants are not arrested for six months. The city also agreed to pay $231,200 to protesters and their lawyers to settle contempt charges against the city.

Lawsuits were filed, arising out of the RNC protests, which will be sorted out in court. Regardless of the outcome, there were several lessons learned.

Once again the time-tested use of marches, demonstrations, and rallies brought attention to the views of those outside the government. As in the past, there were accusations that the police had overreacted, violating the rights of lawful protesters and innocent bystanders. Yet in the end, freedom of assembly had played a vital role in ensuring that the American people participated in a robust, wide-open debate on the future of their country. It was not the first time that had happened in America, and it will certainly not be the last.

7

The Internet Community and the Future of Freedom of Assembly, Association, and Petition

Thomas Jefferson and James Madison could not have imagined the invention of the Internet linking millions of people around the world in a network of instantaneous communications. The founders, however, were keen observers of human nature and understood the deep yearning of people to connect with one another and their instinctive curiosity to learn about each other. These visionaries realized that given the means and opportunity, people of common interests would naturally join together.

It is likely that Jefferson, Madison, and their forward-looking colleagues might have embraced the Internet for its potential to enrich and expand American democracy and to engage vast numbers of people in the exercise of their freedom of assembly, their freedom of association, and their right to petition the government for redress of grievances.

Jefferson wrote, "Whenever the people are well-informed, they can be trusted with their own government." Madison wrote, "Knowledge will forever govern ignorance, and a people who mean to be their own governors must arm themselves with the power which knowledge gives."

The Internet may be perfectly suited not only to equip people with knowledge and information but to serve as a conduit helping them to locate like-minded people with similar interests, whether they be intellectual, political, religious, social, recreational, or anything else.

Americans have traditionally met together at town halls and other public places to socialize and exchange ideas. One wonders if the Internet will change that. *(Library of Congress, Prints and Photographs Division, LC-USF34-036661-D)*

ORIGINS OF THE INTERNET

The Internet was an outgrowth of an internal government communications system known as the Advanced Research Projects Agency Network (ARPANET) developed by the Department of Defense in the late 1960s. One of the developers of ARPANET, J. C. R. Licklider, conceived of a "spirit of community" created by a group of individuals simultaneously sharing information and resources through an interconnected computer system.

THE POWER OF THE INTERNET

Although the Internet has been around in one form or another since the 1970s, it emerged in the 1990s and became a mass phenomenon around 1995 or 1996. In 2000 Democrat Bill Bradley and Republican John McCain used the Internet to build support and raise money for their presidential campaigns. By winter 2003–04, according to the Pew Research Center for the People and the Press, more than 40 million people used the Internet to research or participate in the

THE RULE OF 75 PERCENT

How many years does it take for 75 percent of households in America to acquire new technology? The telephone took 67 years to increase from 1 percent of households to 75 percent. The automobile took 52 years. Radio took 14 years. In 1948, only 1 percent of homes in America had a television set, but eight years later, by 1956, the number had reached 75 percent. (By 1985, the average American had *two* televisions in their home.) For the Internet, it has taken seven years for 75 percent of Americans to get connected.

presidential campaign by looking up news and information, exchanging e-mails, joining discussion groups, or signing petitions.

Recognizing that the Internet is a powerful new means of communication that enhances freedom of expression is one thing, but does the Internet have the capacity to energize freedom of assembly?

Increasingly, the Internet is doing just that, from organizing worldwide antiwar demonstrations to mobilizing people in their own neighborhoods to become active in their communities. The Internet has been of particular help to local organizations, including neighborhood associations, community development corporations, civic-minded business associations, union locals, and grassroots political clubs. The term *NetActivism* has entered the language.

Million Mom March

The Million Mom March (MMM) in 2000 is one example of how the Internet can mobilize people to exercise their freedom of assembly. Prompted by a 1999 incident where a gunman randomly shot at a group of children at a day-care center in Southern California, Donna Dees-Thomases, a politically active New Jersey publicist, established the MMM coalition made up of Handgun Control Inc., the Coalition Against Gun Violence, and the *Bell Campaign,* a grassroots counterpoint to the National Rifle Association founded in 1999. With the goal of promoting gun licensing and registration,

MMM took full advantage of the Internet by developing custom database design, circulating information, and asking people to register for the march. Eventually 1 million people signed up. Not all of them could attend the march, but on May 14, 2000, 750,000 people gathered together on the National Mall in Washington, D.C., with between 150,000 and 200,000 more attending local marches in their home states. And 500,000 responded to an Internet appeal to send special Mother's Day cards, highlighting the campaign.

Partnership for Parks

Partnership for Parks, a public-private partnership in New York City that helps manage and maintain city parks, is another example. The Parks 2001 campaign was an effort to encourage all candidates running for mayor to commit to raising the parks budget to a full 1 percent of total expenditures. Taking full advantage of the Internet, Partnership for Parks built a "greenlist," a database combining the membership and notification lists of many different environmental organizations. Not only did everyone on the greenlist receive e-mail announcements and action alerts, but the technology also allowed those messages to be tailored to each group. Beyond all this, Partnership for Parks used the Internet to get people to attend public meetings and events. Among the various mayoral forums for various important issues held during the campaign, the one on parks got the highest turnout.

Howard Dean

There are many stories about the power of the Internet. One example stands out and is emblematic of the impact the Internet can have on the political life of America.

One of the earliest and most revolutionary uses of the Internet to create a virtual political movement, combining electronic connections with face-to-face assemblies, was the candidacy of Vermont Governor Howard Dean seeking the Democratic nomination in the 2004 presidential election. Little-known nationally (Vermont being the second-smallest state in the union), few gave Dean any chance of getting elected president when in late 2002 he began his run for the White House. One insider told *New York* magazine that Dean's candidacy was "the silliest thing I'd never heard." That critic was his mother.

In January 2003, in Iowa, where the first primary for the Democratic nomination would be held one year later, 82 percent of the voters could not identify Howard Dean, according to a Zogby International Poll. Yet, during the following year, Dean would achieve one of the most astonishing political accomplishments in U.S. history, becoming the front-runner for the nomination of a major political party, ahead of several other better-known candidates, including Senator John Kerry, Representative Richard Gephardt, Senator Joseph Lieberman, and Senator John Edwards. By all counts, Dean could not have accomplished this miraculous achievement without the Internet.

Dean went from virtual obscurity to being a serious contender for president of the United States by building an unprecedented movement over the Internet with the aid of Joe Trippi, an astute and visionary campaign manager. Trippi had seen the potential for the Internet to empower people to join in a participatory democracy. The Dean campaign was able to mobilize hundreds of thousands of supporters in a short period of time and raise millions of dollars in campaign contributions, all over the Internet.

Trippi had been talking about using an early version of the Internet for a political campaign back in 1984. When Arizona Senator John McCain ran for the Republican nomination for president in 2000, McCain used the Internet in his campaign, but the technology was still primitive and very few people had a personal Internet connection.

By the time Trippi joined the Dean campaign in 2003, all that had changed. Due to the popularity of America OnLine, Yahoo!, Amazon.com, eBay, and Google.com, millions of people felt comfortable, and even adept, at using the Internet.

In fact, Trippi discovered that the Dean campaign had already developed on the Internet without anyone at the Dean headquarters knowing anything about it. In a real sense, the Internet community was already exercising its freedom of assembly and freedom of association around the Dean candidacy without any permission or approval from Howard Dean or anyone else.

At the time, a struggling new Web site called Meetup.com gave people with similar interests (such as *Star Trek* or parakeets) an opportunity to meet up with each other and discuss their common interest.

> "[On the Internet,] everything is a community [with the potential of creating] a commons, a town square, a place where people can come together."
>
> —*Joe Trippi*, The Revolution Will Not Be Televised: Democracy, the Internet and the Overthrow of Everything, *2004*

Trippi discovered that without any official coaxing or organizing from Dean headquarters, 432 Dean supporters had already voluntarily met up on Meetup.com to get together to talk about Howard Dean.

As soon as Trippi put a link to Meetup.com on the official Dean for America Web site, suddenly the total jumped to 2,700. Within

---

MEETUP.COM

Scott Heiferman, Peter Kamali, and Matt Meeker created Meetup.com in June 2002 to foster civic participation and restore a sense of community in America following the attacks of September 11, 2001. By fall 2004, close to 2 million people in more than 1,000 cities were using the site to schedule meetings with others interested in everything from poker, Harry Potter, and Elvis to presidential politics to more than 5,000 other topic groups. There are 254 groups devoted to *Star Trek,* with 2,401 members; 211 groups of Mustang owners, with 809 members; and 126 groups of Ayn Rand enthusiasts, with 646 members. During the 2004 presidential election, 10,000 users signed up for Republican Party groups, 67,000 signed up for Democratic Party meet-ups, and almost 5,000 supporters signed up for Ralph Nader meet-ups.

Heiferman said that Meetup.com was founded to figure out how "we can use the Internet to get people off the Internet." Meetup.com connects people with common interests and arranges meetings in local neighborhoods for more than 30,000 groups. New people can log on to the site and find the nearest meeting. Beyond such local meetings, Meetup.com played a critical role in April 2003 in mobilizing participants for the March for Women's Lives, an abortion rights demonstration, that drew as many as 800,000 people to Washington, D.C. For creating Meetup.com, Heiferman received the 2004 Innovator of the Year Award from Massachusetts Institute of Technology's scientific journal *Technology Review.* The award is given to individuals under 35 years old whose innovative work "[has] the promise or the potential to transform existing businesses and fields of technology or create new ones."

weeks, the number of people interested in meeting up to talk about Dean had increased to 8,000. Eventually, more than 190,000 people signed up to join the Dean meet-up phenomenon. Another 170,000 got involved through Trippi's specialized version of Meetup.com called GetLocal, which allowed people to enter a zip code and find the nearest Dean meeting. Organizers could use it to locate people to distribute campaign literature or organize a house party.

Nothing like this had ever happened before. More than 360,000 people were connecting with each other over the Internet for the common purpose of becoming active in a political campaign. And they were not just sitting at home at a computer, isolated by themselves. They were utilizing the new technology of the Internet to locate like-minded others and then meet them face to face to advance their shared goals. Many have recognized the Internet as a revolutionary technology to expand freedom of speech. What the Dean movement proved is that the Internet was also well-suited to enhance freedom of assembly and freedom of association, building a virtual community where none had existed before.

Dean officially announced his candidacy on June 23, 2003. It was the first political campaign announcement in U.S. history carried live over the Internet, with 30,000 people linked up at about 400 events across the country, ranging, as the Dean Web site proclaimed, "from half-a-dozen people watching the speech and eating cake at the Bodes General Store in rural Abiquiu, New Mexico, to more than 1,200 people packed in the San Francisco Hyatt Regency."

Eventually, Howard Dean did not win the 2004 Democratic nomination. But his Internet campaign added a dynamic chapter to the history of freedom of assembly.

BUILDING AN INTERNET COMMUNITY

The Internet has become a vital new and inexpensive tool for organizing rallies, marches, and demonstrations. Before the Internet, organizers had to print posters and photocopy fliers announcing upcoming events, which were then distributed by hand or posted on bulletin boards in dormitories and classroom buildings, on telephone poles, or in other public places. Beginning in the 1960s the practice of "tabling" sprang up on college campuses and shopping malls, where activists would set up card tables to distribute political literature (a practice that continues to this day). Organizations were dependent on occasional announcements on local radio stations and the time-honored method of word-of-mouth to publicize upcoming marches, demonstrations, and events.

The Internet changed all that. New digital and electronic information and communication technologies created a new environment allowing organizations to communicate cheaply and quickly, unconstrained by time or distance. As its basic level—e-mail—the Internet allows a single organizer to simultaneously alert hundreds, even thousands of people to take action, whether to attend a meeting, participate in a rally, march, or demonstration (next week or that very day), or to send a letter or make a phone call. At the next level, Web-based chat rooms and bulletin boards created online space for interactive conversations—virtual meetings—avoiding the time and expense of face-to-face meetings. Internet mailing lists and newsgroups became valuable tools to reach vast numbers of people instantaneously.

ListServe, an e-mail list management software developed in 1986, became a leading brand that together with other software systems delivers millions of messages to millions of Internet users every day. An untold number of announcements, fundraising appeals, calls to action, and alerts have been communicated over such e-mail lists, expanding the reach of new and small political organizations far beyond anything ever imagined by political activists in the 1960s and 1970s.

The center of most electronic political organizing is the Web site. Here, with varying levels of sophistication, groups can display a description of who they are, what they stand for, what they are doing, and how one can join them or donate money. Web sites often contain calendars of events with dates, times, speakers, and directions. Position papers, press releases, public statements, key documents, legal pleadings, photographs, and other information can be posted, archived, and accessed. Graphics and text for protest signs can be downloaded in minutes. Many Web sites contain links to other related Web sites allowing interested parties to easily see what other organizations are planning.

In 1993, the Rand Corporation predicted that the "revolutionary forces of the future may consist increasingly of widespread multi-organizational networks that have no particular national identity, claim to arise from civil society and include aggressive groups and individuals who are keenly adept at using advanced technology for communications." For grassroots political organizations, unions, environmental groups, religious congregations, and others, the future Rand envisioned is here. No one can fix a single date when that took place, but spring 2003 will be recorded as a pivotal moment when the Internet began to play a central role in political organizing. With the U.S. government preparing to go to war in Iraq, hundreds of Web sites, many cross-linked to maximize their total impact, urged people in the United States and around the world to take action to stop the war. Journalist Cynthia Webb, in the *Washington Post* on March 11, 2003, wrote that the "Internet is allowing antiwar groups to communicate nationwide and across the globe in ways hardly possible during any other conflict in American history."

In February 2003, MoveOn.com (www.moveon.org) and the Win Without War Coalition (www.winwithoutwarus.org) organized a "Virtual March" on Washington, D.C., prompting 85,000 people to call members of Congress and send e-mails and faxes, resulting in what is believed to be the largest single online protest in American history. Antiwar groups such as Not in Our Name (www.notinourname.net), International ANSWER (Act Now to Stop War and End Racism at www.internationalanswer.org), the National Network to End the War Against Iraq (www.endthewar. org), Education for Peace in Iraq Center (www.peacepledge.org), Cities for Peace (www.patriotsforpeace.org), and Interfaith Communities United for Justice and Peace (www.icujp.org) used its Web site and e-mail lists to drum up attendance for rallies and demonstrations planned in Washington, D.C., San Francisco, New York City, and elsewhere.

But the genius of the Internet is that is not restricted to any particular political viewpoint or party. Consequently, in spring 2003 there were many Web sites supporting Bush's plans to attack Iraq. Grassfire.net (www.grassfire.net) condemned antiwar groups for attacking "the president and his desires to free the world from the grip of terror" and asked people to sign a petition supporting Bush. Free Republic (www.freerepublic.com) promoted rallies in support of U.S. policies on Iraq to counter the antiwar protests that were popping up all across the nation. "Form a group, grab your signs, unfurl the flag and prepare to support your country!" From Patriots for the Defense of America (www.defenseofamerica.org) to Victory over Terrorism (www.avot.org), from Leatherneck.com (www.leatherneck.com) to the Foundation for the Defense of Democracies (www.defenddemocracy.org), supporters of the government did not leave it to the government to build support for the war. On all sides of this momentous decision involving war and peace—the first war of the 21st century—the Internet played a critical role in educating and mobilizing supporters and opponents alike.

The Internet appears to be attracting a particular segment of society that once alerted to a cause or issue is more likely to exercise their rights to assemble, associate, and petition the government for redress of grievances. According to the Institute for Politics, Democracy & the Internet, those they call "Online Political Citizens" (OPCs) are seven times more likely than average citizens to serve as opinion leaders among their friends, relatives, and colleagues. While generally 10 percent of Americans qualify as "Influentials" (those who serve as opinion leaders) the institute's study found that 69 percent of OPCs are "Influentials."

The Internet is not without its disadvantages as an engine of democracy. Since the poor, minorities, and the elderly often lack access to or are unfamiliar with this new technology, the Internet offers greater opportunities for wealthier, middle-class people. Additionally, the Internet has become divided into highly specialized, narrow, single-issue sites, which tends to lead to what author and law professor Cass Sunstein calls "cyberbalkanization." In cyberbalkanization activists only interact with those who already agree with them, creating an "echo chamber" rather than a wide-open, robust debate.

Howard Rheingold, in his books *The Virtual Community* (1993) and *Smart Mobs* (2003), predicted that computers and other advanced technology would foster community building, transform cultures, and "change the way people meet, mate, work, fight, buy, sell, govern and create." According to Joe Trippi, on the Internet "everything is a community." He predicts that Internet communities "will not be geographic but will be constructed of people with similar interest, aesthetics, and beliefs."

THE INTERNET FACILITATES THE RIGHT TO PETITION

Separate and apart from the Internet's role in enhancing freedom of assembly and freedom of association, it has become a powerful, low-cost, and efficient means for people to petition the government for redress of grievances. Indeed, it is tailor made to assist vast numbers of people to send individual messages to elected officials and participate in organized letter-writing campaigns. Organizations big and small have become adept at creating user-friendly Web pages where people in a matter of minutes can insert their name, address, e-mail address, and other relevant information and immediately dispatch a message to the president of the United States, a U.S. senator, a governor, a mayor, or a school-board member. With equal ease people can sign on to petitions urging everything from ending a war to installing a traffic light.

From individual e-mail accounts people can compose a personal letter asking an elected official to address an issue, from a missing Social Security check to reforming the entire Social Security system. The staffs of elected officials report that they log in every e-mail (as well as every letter and telephone call) and do their best to respond to the problems raised.

A wide array of Web sites help facilitate the right of petition. PetitionOnline (www.petitiononline.com) provides "free online hosting of public petitions for responsible public advocacy." Claiming to have collected more than 20 million signatures, the site has thousands of active petitions dealing with everything from asking Congress to ensure that nothing happens to a U.S. Marine suspected of killing a wounded insurgent in Iraq to prohibiting black bear hunting in New Jersey to seeking justice for victims of the chemical Agent Orange used during the Vietnam War to asking Congress to investigate voting problems in the 2004 presidential election.

PetitionOnline proclaims that it gives people "the ancient methods of *grass roots* democracy combined with the latest digital network communications, running live and free 24 hours a day." PetitionOnline reports that some petitions have received more than 100,000 signatures in a week. Organizations which do not have the resources or know-how to gather signatures on their own Web sites can put their petitions at PetitionOnline and then put a link on their Web site. Organizations without a Web site can simply publicize their petition by e-mail or other conventional methods. PetitionOnline states that "in a world with many powerful organizations, both private and governmental, responsible forms of collective grassroots expressions are more important than ever. And we believe the Internet can facilitate this kind of participatory democracy."

The Petition Site (www.thepetitionsite.com) is an example of online petitioning focusing primarily on protecting the environment. It proudly displays its success stories, including the Heritage Forest campaign, an alliance of conservationists, wildlife advocates, clergy, educators, scientists, and others working together to protect the National Forests, that collected over 40,000 public signatures and comments to the U.S. Forestry Service demanding special protection for America's national forests from timber, mining, and oil companies and the Arctic National Wildlife Refuge campaign, which collected over 100,000 comments that were delivered to key senators urging them to vote against drilling in the Arctic.

Conservative Petition.Com (www.conservativepetitions.com) asks, "Are you outraged by what liberals are doing to America? Heard enough and want to make a difference? Then this tremendous resource is for you." This site carries petitions urging Congress to censure 13 Democrats in the House of Representatives for calling on the United Nations to monitor the 2004 presidential election and urging Congress to prohibit federal courts from reviewing actions by the states, such as allowing the posting of the Ten Commandments in public buildings.

WebPetitions.Com (www.webpetitions.com) contains thousands of petitions that have been submitted since 2000, covering everything from legalizing marijuana to supporting a bill in Rhode Island to give adopted children access to their original birth certificate.

Petitions.Org (www.petitions.org), established in 1999, is a nonpartisan, viewpoint-neutral site that says petitions "can and do influence governments and businesses across the globe" and can "turn beliefs into action." The site proclaims that "the right to sign and distribute [p]etitions is a fundamental human right," stating as its motto: "Harnessing the power of the web to breathe new life into one of the oldest, most effective tools of democracy; and enabling all people—liberal and conservative, radical and moderate—to seek change."

Contacting the Congress (www.visi.com/juan/congress) is an up-to-date database with congressional contact information where people can find out who represents them in Congress, contact their representatives by e-mail, discover on which committees their representatives serve, and link to other related sites that contain voting histories, political news, state government information, and Senate and House schedules and activities. Since the site was established in

1994, more than 3,391,000 people have logged on. The site was created by Juan Cabanela, who is currently an assistant professor of physics and astronomy at Saint Cloud University, in Minnesota, and is available in both English and Spanish. Cabanela started the site because he wanted to contact his Congress member to complain that a manned space station was being built at the expense of other science.

MoveOn.com (www.moveon.com) has had an important impact on transforming the Internet into a powerful vehicle for democratic participation. Founded in 1998 to oppose the impeachment of President Bill Clinton ("There are more important things facing the country, so let's move on"), MoveOn has emerged as a dynamic e-mail-driven force which circulates information, raises money, and makes it easy for people to sign petitions and send messages on urgent issues.

By late 2004, MoveOn claimed that with more than 2,750,000 online activists, it was "one of the most effective and responsive outlets for democratic participation available today." MoveOn describes itself as a "catalyst for a new kind of *grass roots* involvement, supporting busy but concerned citizens in finding their political voice" by building "electronic advocacy groups" on issues such as "campaign finance, environment and energy issues, media consolidation and the Iraq war."

Recent MoveOn victories listed on its Web site include generating 500,000 signatures and 20,000 phone calls within 48 hours to help defeat a constitutional amendment prohibiting marriage between same-sex couples and gathering 375,000 online activists to oppose proposed rules by the Federal Communications Commission that would have allowed fewer corporations to control more radio and television stations.

The separate MoveOn Political Action Committee raised more than $2 million from 10,000 contributors for key congressional campaigns in the 2000 election and more than $3.5 million in the 2002 election.

Joan Blades, one of the founders of MoveOn, is optimistic about the impact of the Internet on democratic participation. "It's still very experimental. . . . People want it, crave it. We amplify each other's voices when we come together . . . and people love it. So many people have felt cut out of the conversation. The MoveOn members, many of whom were not active, found it tremendously satisfying. It's exactly what they wanted to be doing."

THE FUTURE

Only time will tell whether the Internet will enrich freedom of assembly, association, and petition. There are signs that the general public would support such a movement. In a 2003 survey by the First Amendment Center, 95 percent agreed that individuals should be allowed to express unpopular opinions, and two-thirds supported the right of any group to hold a rally for a cause, even if that cause is offensive to others.

Should the impact of the Internet on freedom of assembly only be judged in terms of getting people away from the computer and out on the street where they can meet face to face with like-minded allies? Instead of assessing the Internet's role in the history of freedom of assembly by looking backward to the old ways in which advocates have assembled to advance their cause, one perhaps should be looking forward to examine whether the Internet itself is a brand-new forum for the exercise of freedom of assembly.

The Internet instantaneously can assemble hundreds, thousands, even hundreds of thousands of people to respond to an immediate call to action, to hear and see speeches, to gather information, and to take action, all without the expense, delay, and inconvenience of traveling to a meeting, march, rally, for demonstration across town or across the world.

Cyber-assemblies offer the promise of greater participation to those who cannot afford the time or expense of leaving work or family to attend face-to-face gatherings. They allow people to join in events that are being broadcast by streaming video in real time. Other people can participate by time-shifting, thereby experiencing the meeting, march, rally, or demonstration whenever they are available. And everyone who participates can immediately respond by making an online contribution or sending a message to an elected official or a letter to the editor.

No one is predicting that the virtual right of assembly over the Internet will entirely replace face-to-face gatherings. Movies and television have not replaced the immediacy of live theater. There is no substitute for being physically present and appreciating the reality of a live rally, march, or demonstrations. Nor is there any substitute for the way that massive gatherings attract public and media attention.

The Internet represents a new, dynamic technology that is transforming society and the way people exercise their constitutional

Freedom of association is fully realized when people join together to pursue common goals. *(Library of Congress, Prints and Photographs Division, LC-USF34-110061-C)*

rights. The yearning of people to join together in common enterprises for the sake of personal development and the advancement of the human race is deeply felt. The need to assemble, associate, and seek to make things better is a powerful human trait that will continue to motivate people in every walk of life.

Regardless of the impact of the Internet, the right to peaceably assembly, freedom of association, and the right to petition will thrive whenever and wherever there is a cause to be championed. The Internet joins television, radio, motion pictures, and the printing press as a means of communication that supplements what is happening in the streets.

No technology will replace the immediate impact of people meeting face to face, marching together, demonstrating together, organizing together, associating together, lobbying together—doing it all together as so many have before them. So long as society, and by extension the courts and elected officials, respect and uphold the right to assemble, associate, and petition, American democracy will retain its vibrancy and its hope and will remain a government of the people, by the people, and for the people.

Glossary

abolitionist   A person who favors the abolition of any institution, especially African-American slavery.

activism   The use of direct, often confrontational action, such as a demonstration or strike, in opposition to or support of a cause.

advocacy   The act of pleading or arguing in favor of something, such as a cause, idea, or policy; active support.

allegiance   Loyalty or the obligation of loyalty, as to a nation or cause.

alliance   A close association of nations or other groups, formed to advance common interests or causes.

amendments   The process of formally altering or adding to a document or record.

antiwar protests   Demonstrations, marches, rallies, or other public activities organized to oppose a particular war or war in general.

autonomy   The condition or quality of being autonomous; independence. Autonomy is also self-government or the right of self-government; self-determination. It can also mean a self-governing state, community, or group.

baron   A British nobleman of the lowest rank, holding his rights and title directly from a king or another feudal superior. A baron may have great wealth, power, and influence in a specified sphere of activity.

bigotry   An intolerant attitude, state of mind, or behavior based on bias and prejudice toward people of a particular race, ethnicity, religion, or social group.

bill   Statute in draft before it becomes law.

125

bill of rights   A formal summary of the rights and liberties considered essential to a people or group of people. The U.S. Bill of Rights are the first 10 amendments to the U.S. Constitution, added in 1791 to protect certain rights of citizens.

birth control   Voluntary limitation or control of the number of children conceived, especially by planned use of contraceptive techniques.

blacklist   A list of persons or organizations that have incurred disapproval or suspicion or are to be boycotted or otherwise penalized.

blind faith   Belief without true understanding, perception, or discrimination.

blog   A personal Web site that provides updated headlines and news articles of other sites that are of interest to the user; it also may include journal entries, commentaries, and recommendations compiled by the user.

boycott   To abstain from or act together in abstaining from using, buying, or dealing with a product or service as an expression of protest or disfavor or as a means of coercion.

card-carrying members   An ironic expression applied to real, suspected or accused members of the Communist Party, conferring upon them the bourgeois respectability of a businessman.

charter   A document issued by a king, legislature, or other authority creating a public or private corporation, such as a city, college, or bank, and defining its privileges and purposes.

civil disobedience   Refusal to obey civil laws in an effort to induce change in governmental policy or legislation, characterized by the use of passive resistance or other nonviolent means.

civil liberties   Fundamental individual rights, such as freedom of speech, press, religion, and assembly, protected by law against unwarranted governmental or other interference.

civil rights   The rights belonging to an individual, especially the fundamental freedoms and privileges guaranteed by the thirteenth and fourteenth Amendments to the U.S. Constitution and by subsequent acts of Congress, including civil liberties, due process, equal protection of the laws, and freedom from discrimination.

civil war   A war between different sections or parties of the same country or nation.

colonial assemblies   The deliberative bodies that sought to exercise legislative powers in the original American colonies.

colony   A company of people transplanted from their mother country to a remote province or country and remaining subject to the jurisdiction of the parent state (for example, the 13 British colonies before the development of America).

communists   Members of a Marxist-Leninist party; supporters of such a party or movement.

confederation   The act of forming or becoming part of a group, especially of states or nations, united for a common purpose.

congregate   To come together in a group, crowd, or assembly.

constitution   The act or document composing, setting up, or establishing a system of fundamental laws and principles that prescribes the nature, functions, and limits of a government or another institution.

The Crown   A king or queen.

debate   Contention in words or arguments; discussion for the purpose of elucidating truth or influencing action.

Declaration of Independence   The declaration of the Congress of the Thirteen United States of America, on July 4, 1776, by which they formally declared that the colonies were free and independent states, not subject to the government of Great Britain.

deliberate   Done with or marked by full consciousness of the nature and effects; intentional.

democracy   Government by the people, exercised either directly or through elected representatives.

demonstrations   A public display of group opinion, as by a rally or march.

deported   To exile; to send into banishment.

discrimination   Unfair treatment of a person or group on the basis of prejudice.

disinformation   Deliberately misleading information announced publicly or leaked by a government or especially by an intelligence agency in order to influence public opinion or the government of another nation.

dissent   To differ in opinion or feeling; disagree; the refusal to conform to the authority or doctrine of an established church; nonconformity. A dissent can also mean a justice's refusal to concur with the opinion of a majority, as on a higher court.

dissident   One who disagrees; a dissenter.

distrain   To seize and hold property to compel payment or reparation, as of debts.

distress   To hold the property of a person against the payment of debts.

divine right   A doctrine that kings and queens derive their right to rule directly from a higher spiritual power (such as God) and are accountable only to that entity.

due process   An established course for judicial proceedings or other governmental activities designed to safeguard the legal rights of the individual.

Equal Rights Amendment (ERA)   A proposed amendment to the U.S. Constitution, which was never ratified, guaranteeing that rights would not be denied on the basis of sex.

ethnicity   A quality or affiliation resulting from racial or cultural ties.

executive   The chief officer of a government, state, or political division; the branch of government charged with putting into effect a country's laws and the administering of its functions.

First Amendment   An amendment to the Constitution of the United States guaranteeing the right of free expression, including the right to peaceably assemble, freedom of the press, freedom of religion, and freedom of speech.

forefathers   Ancestors; persons who are from an earlier time and have originated or contributed to a common tradition shared by a particular group.

founders   Individuals who establish something or formulate the basis for something. Those who established the United States of America under the Declaration of Independence, the U.S. Constitution, and the Bill of Rights are referred to as the country's Founders.

freedom of assembly   The right to assemble peaceably and to petition the government for redress of grievances; guaranteed for example by the First Amendment to the U.S. Constitution.

freedom of association   The right guaranteed by the First Amendment to the U.S. Constitution through court interpretations to join with others either in personal relationships or as part of a group usually having a common viewpoint or purpose and often exercising the right to assemble and to free speech.

freedom of speech   The right, as guaranteed by the First Amendment to the U.S. Constitution to express ideas and opinions free of government restrictions based on content.

freedom of the press   The right, guaranteed by the First Amendment to the U.S. Constitution, to write, publish, disseminate, and broadcast, ideas, opinions, and information in newspapers, books, magazines, radio, television, and other forms of communication.

Freedom Rider   One of an interracial group of civil rights activists in the early 1960s who rode buses through parts of the southern United States for the purpose of challenging racial segregation.

Freedom Schools   A program of education training students and activists in the principles of nonviolence and passive resistance during the Civil Rights Movement in the United States in the 1950s and 1960s.

free speech   The right to express any opinion in public without censorship or restraint by the government.

free speech zones   Limited areas set aside by police or local officials restricting freedom of speech and freedom of assembly to only those areas.

globalization   To make global or worldwide in scope or application; growth to a global or worldwide scale.

grass-roots   People seeking social and political change at a local level rather than elected officials or certain elites within the established major political parties.

guilt by association   The attribution of guilt, without proof, to individuals because the people they associate with are guilty.

House of Representatives   The lower house of the U.S. Congress and of most state legislatures.

identity   The set of behavioral or personal characteristics by which an individual is recognizable as a member of a group.

immigrants   A person who leaves one country to settle permanently in another.

independence   The state or quality of being free from dependence; exemption from reliance on, or control by, others; self-subsistence or maintenance; direction of one's own affairs without interference.

indictment   A written statement charging a party with the commission of a crime or other offense, drawn up by a prosecuting attorney and found and presented by a grand jury.

industrialization   The transformation of an economy from one dependent on agriculture and family farms to the production and distribution of goods and services on a large scale using factories, machines, and technology.

injunction   A court order prohibiting a party from a specific course of action.

Internet   An interconnected system of electronic networks that link computers around the world to facilitate data transmission and exchange of information.

intolerance   Refusal to allow to others the enjoyment of their opinions, chosen modes of worship, and the like; want of patience and forbearance; illiberality; bigotry.

Jim Crow laws   The systematic practice of discriminating against and segregating black people, especially as practiced in the American South from the end of Reconstruction to the mid-20th century.

judicial   Of, relating to, or proper to courts of law or to the administration of justice.

legislative   Having the power or performing the function of legislating belonging to the branch of government that is charged with such powers as making laws, levying and collecting taxes, and making financial appropriations.

liberation   The act or process of trying to achieve equal rights and status and the removal of oppressive laws or conditions.

liberty   Freedom from external (as governmental) restraint, compulsion, or interference in engaging in the pursuits or conduct of one's choice to the extent that they are lawful and not harmful to others; enjoyment of the rights enjoyed by others in a society free of arbitrary or unreasonable limitation or interference.

litigation   To contest in legal proceedings.

lobbying   A group of persons engaged in trying to influence legislators or other public officials in favor of a specific cause.

loyalists   One who maintains loyalty to an established government, political party, or sovereign, especially during war or revolutionary change.

march   An organized walk, as for a public cause.

McCarthyism   The practice of publicizing accusations of political disloyalty or subversion with insufficient regard to evidence; unscrupulously accusing people of disloyalty, as by saying they were Communists.

Meetup   A practice developed over the Internet in 2003 connecting people of common interests and alerting them to places to get together in their community.

monarch   A sole or supreme ruler; the highest ruler; an emperor, king, queen, prince, or chief.

nationalism   Devotion to the interests or culture of one's nation.

Nazism   The ideology and practice of the Nazis, in Germany in the 1930s and 1940s, especially the policy of racist nationalism, national expansion, and state control of the economy.

New Deal   The programs and policies to promote economic recovery and social reform introduced during the 1930s by President Franklin D. Roosevelt.

nongovernmental organizations (NGOs)   Organizations that are not part of the local, state, or federal government.

nonviolence   The doctrine, policy, or practice of rejecting violence in favor of peaceful tactics as a means of gaining political objectives; abstaining (on principle) from the use of violence.

pacifists   The belief that disputes between nations should and can be settled peacefully; opposition to war or violence as a means of resolving disputes.

pamphlet   An unbound printed work, usually with a paper cover; a short essay or treatise, usually on a current topic, published without a binding.

patriotism   Love of and devotion to one's country.

peaceably   Inclined or disposed to promoting calm, accomplished without violence or threat of violence.

peace treaty   A treaty between nations to cease hostilities.

permit   To allow the doing of an act; consent to; authorize; a document or certificate giving permission to do something; a license or warrant.

persecution   Punishment or harassment on the basis of race, religion, or political opinion in one's country of origin; the infliction of loss, pain, or death for adherence to a particular creed or mode of worship.

petition   A formal written document requesting a right or benefit from a person or group in authority; a formal written application requesting a court for a specific judicial action, such as a petition for appeal.

picket   A person or group of persons stationed outside a place of employment, usually during a strike, to express grievance or protest and to discourage entry by nonstriking employees or customers.

pilgrim   A religious devotee who journeys to a shrine or sacred place. English Separatists who founded the colony of Plymouth in New England in 1620 were known as Pilgrims.

preamble   A preliminary statement, especially the introduction to a formal document or constitution that serves to explain its purpose.

prejudices   An adverse judgment or opinion formed beforehand or without knowledge or examination of the facts.

privacy   The quality or condition of being secluded from the presence or view of others; the state of being free from unsanctioned intrusion.

proclamations   An official public announcement, given orally or in writing.

protests   Formal declarations of disapproval or objection issued by a concerned person, group, or organization; an individual or collective gesture or display of disapproval.

racism   The belief that race accounts for differences in human character or ability and that a particular race is superior to others; discrimination or prejudice based on race.

rank-and-file   The people who form the major portion of a group, organization, or society, excluding the leaders and officers.

redress of grievances   To correct or solve a problem or complaint.

remonstrance   An expression of protest, complaint, or reproof, especially a formal statement of grievances.

repealed   To revoke or rescind, especially by an official or formal act.

repression   The act of denying someone, a group of persons, or an entire society the rights and privileges they deserve.

restraining order   A court order prohibiting a party from a specific act.

restraint of trade   An action or condition that tends to prevent or hamper free competition in business, as the creation of a monopoly or the limiting of a market.

searches and seizures   To enter private property and take items into custody as evidence of a crime, usually carried out by law enforcement officers.

segregation   The act, process, policy, or practice of separating people of different races, classes, or ethnic groups, as in schools, housing, and public or commercial facilities, especially as a form of discrimination.

self-government   A government of the people, for the people, and by the people.

senate   An assembly or a council of citizens having the highest deliberative and legislative functions in a government. The upper house of the U.S. Congress, to which two members are elected from each state by popular vote for a six-year term, is called the Senate.

sit-in   An organized protest demonstration in which participants seat themselves in a public place and refuse to move; the act of occupying the seats or an area of a segregated establishment to protest racial discrimination.

slavery   The state of one bound in servitude as the property of a master or household.

state action   An action that is either taken directly by the government or bears a sufficient connection to the government to be attributed to it.

states' rights   All rights not delegated to the federal government by the Constitution nor denied by it to the states.

stereotypes   A conventional and oversimplified conception, opinion, or image; one that is regarded as embodying or conforming to a set image or type.

stigmatized   To characterize or brand as disgraceful or ignominious; to set a mark of disgrace on; to brand with some mark of reproach or infamy.

strike   A cessation of work by employees in support of demands made on their employer, as for higher pay or improved conditions.

subversive   Intended or serving to overthrow or undermine an established government, a person who advocates or is regarded as advocating subversion.

Supreme Court   The highest federal court in the United States consisting of nine justices and having final say in interpreting federal laws and the U.S. Constitution.

traitor   One who betrays one's country, a cause, or a trust; one who commits treason.

tyranny   A form of government in which the ruler is an absolute dictator (not restricted by a constitution, laws, or opposition).

unalienable   Incapable of being repudiated or transferred to another; not to be separated, given away, or taken away; also: inalienable.

unconstitutional   Not in accord with the principles set forth in the constitution of a nation or state.

union   A combination so formed, especially an alliance or confederation of people, parties, or political entities for mutual interest or benefit.

white supremacist   One who believes that white people are racially superior to others and should therefore dominate society.

witch hunt   An investigation carried out ostensibly to uncover subversive activities but actually used to harass and undermine those with differing views.

Chronology

1215

- King John signs the Magna Carta at Runnymede, England, guaranteeing certain personal rights and agreeing to the formation of the Grand Council, perhaps the earliest recognition of freedom of assembly.

1620

- The Mayflower Compact is signed by the Pilgrims on their voyage to America.

1689

- The British Bill of Rights guarantees the right to petition the king as one of the rights of the people.

1765

- South Carolina Assembly protests against taxes being imposed without the consent of the people.

1765

- Congress of All Colonies meets in New York to declare the "natural and inherent rights" of all persons in America.

1768

- Massachusetts Legislature denounces the Townshend Acts as "taxation without representation."

1773

◆ Rebellious colonists stage the Boston Tea Party, dumping chests of tea into Boston Harbor to protest oppressive British import taxes.

1774

◆ The First Continental Congress meets in Philadelphia.

1775

◆ The American Revolution begins at the Massachusetts towns of Lexington and Concord.

1776

◆ Thomas Paine publishes the influential political pamphlet *Common Sense,* treating Americans as a distinct people, deserving to rule themselves.
◆ Second Continental Congress meets in Philadelphia.
◆ The Declaration of Independence is signed in Philadelphia, citing among other grounds for separating from England the fact that King George III arbitrarily dissolved the colonial legislatures and that the colonists "repeated petitions have been answered only by repeated injury."

1777

◆ The Daughters of Liberty stage the Boston Coffee Party boycotting British goods to protest the exorbitant price of imported coffee.

1787

◆ The Constitutional Convention meeting in Philadelphia adopts the U.S. Constitution but rejects a call for a bill of rights.

1789

◆ The first Congress meets in New York and adopts the Bill of Rights, including the First Amendment, which, among other things, guarantees the right to "peaceably assemble" and the right "to petition the government for redress of grievances."

1791

◆ The Bill of Rights, including the First Amendment, is ratified and becomes part of the U.S. Constitution.

1824

- The first known strike of women factory workers occurs at Pawtucket, Rhode Island, where 202 women refused to work in protest over a wage cut and longer hours.

1834

- A strike of young women in Lowell, Massachusetts, occurs, during which one leader speaks in favor of rights for women and against "monetary aristocracy."

1835

- Massive labor strikes are held in the eastern part of the United States, including Philadelphia, where 50 different organized trade unions demand a 10-hour work day.
- Frederick Douglass, a slave in Baltimore and future leader of the abolition movement, escapes from bondage at age 21.

1844

- Female Labor Reform Association is founded in Lowell, Massachusetts.

1848

- The first Women's Rights Convention, organized by Elizabeth Cady Stanton and Lucretia Mott, convenes in Seneca Falls, New York.

1864

- Congress receives a total of 400,000 signatures on petitions urging legislation to abolish slavery.

1872

- Susan B. Anthony is arrested, convicted, and fined in Rochester, New York, for voting in the presidential election.

1909

- A massive strike occurs in New York among 15,000 shirtwaist workers, almost all women, with another 5,000 joining them the next day.

1911

◆ The Triangle Shirtwaist fire kills 146 people, mostly immigrant women, prompting a massive march of 350,000 people protesting unsafe working conditions.

1917

◆ Congress enacts the Espionage Act under which dissidents and opponents of World War I are later punished for holding rallies and giving speeches.

1919–20

◆ The Federal Bureau of Investigations (FBI) and the Department of Justice conduct a series of raids in more than 33 cities, seeking subversives; known as the "Palmer Raids," named after Attorney General A. Mitchell Palmer.

1920

◆ Authorities obtain a court injunction prohibiting demonstrations and union meetings sponsored by the American Civil Liberties Union (ACLU).

1923

◆ Renowned writer Upton Sinclair is arrested in San Pedro, California, for reading the First Amendment at a rally in support of striking dock workers and members of the Industrial Workers of the World (IWW).

1932

◆ Congress passes the Norris–La Guardia Act, restricting labor injunctions that had previously prevented unions from striking.

1935

◆ Congress passes the Wagner Act, ensuring workers the right to organize unions of their own choosing.

1938

◆ Congress establishes the House Un-American Activities Committee (HUAC) to investigate Communists in the labor movement and later the motion picture and television industries.

1939

◆ In *Hague v. CIO,* the U.S. Supreme Court upholds freedom of assembly by declaring streets and parks a "public forum" protected by the First Amendment.

1940

◆ In *Thornhill v. Alabama,* the U.S. Supreme Court rules that peaceful picketing is protected by the First Amendment.

1942

◆ President Franklin D. Roosevelt issues Executive Order 9066, under which 120,000 Japanese Americans are incarcerated for the duration of World War II, without being charged or convicted of any crimes.

1947

◆ President Harry S. Truman signs Executive Order 9835, creating the Federal Loyalty Program denying employment to anyone believed to be "disloyal" to the government.

1950

◆ Congress enacts the McCarran Act, requiring Communist and "Communist-action" organizations to register with the Subversive Activities Control Board.

1951

◆ In *Dennis v. United States,* the U.S. Supreme Court upholds the Smith Act, making it a crime to belong to the Communist Party.

1953

◆ Senator Joseph McCarthy launches an investigation of Communist influence in the U.S. military, giving rise to accusations of "witch hunting" and "McCarthyism."

1955

◆ Rosa Parks defies segregation on public buses in Montgomery, Alabama, launching the Civil Rights movement.

1958

- In *NAACP v. Alabama,* the U.S. Supreme Court rules that organizations have a constitutional right to keep the names and addresses of their members private.

1960

- Students in Greensboro, North Carolina, defy segregated lunch counters by staging "sit-ins."

1961

- Federal Bureau of Investigations (FBI) launches a secret and massive undercover campaign to disrupt the civil rights activities of Dr. Martin Luther King, Jr.
- Congress of Racial Equality (CORE) organizes "freedom rides" to force compliance with recent desegregation rulings of the U.S. Supreme Court.

1963

- Civil rights activists launch Project Confrontation in Birmingham, Alabama, to protest segregation.
- The March on Washington, D.C., brings 250,000 people to the nation's capitol to hear Martin Luther King, Jr., give his historic "I Have a Dream" speech.
- In *Edwards v. South Carolina,* the U.S. Supreme Court upholds the right of peaceful protesters to march to the South Carolina statehouse carrying antisegregation signs.
- In *NAACP v. Button,* the U.S. Supreme Court rules that the involvement of organizations such as the NAACP in public-interest litigation is constitutionally protected under the rights of expression and association.

1964

- The Civil Rights Act of 1964, prohibiting discrimination in public accommodations, is signed by President Lyndon Johnson.

1965

- Civil rights leaders and activists try to march from Selma to Montgomery, Alabama, but are stopped by state troopers.

1967

- In *U.S. v. Robel,* the U.S. Supreme Court holds that membership in an organization having both lawful and unlawful ends cannot serve as the basis for imposing guilt.

1969

- In *Shuttlesworth v. Birmingham,* the U.S. Supreme Court strikes down as unconstitutional a licensing scheme that allowed local officials to arbitrarily grant or deny permits to hold public demonstrations.
- A massive march against the Vietnam War, with more than 500,000 demonstrators, is held in Washington, D.C.

1970

- Amid widespread demonstrations at hundreds of college campuses across the country, at Kent State University in Ohio, National Guardsmen kill four students and wound nine others.

1972

- The Equal Rights Amendment, prohibiting discrimination against women, is approved by the Senate and House of Representatives but is never ratified.

1977

- Efforts by local officials in Skokie, Illinois, to prevent American Nazis from marching through this predominately Jewish community in which resides many survivors of the Holocaust, result in court decisions affirming the American Nazis's freedom of assembly.

1980

- In *Brown v. Gilnes,* the U.S. Supreme Court holds that base commanders could prevent military personnel from sending a petition to Congress.

1983

- In *U.S. v. Grace,* the U.S. Supreme Court overturns a federal law prohibiting picketing and distributing leaflets on the steps of the court's own building.

1987

+ In *Rotary International v. Rotary Club of Duarte,* the U.S. Supreme Court upholds a California law that prevented Rotary International from excluding women from membership.

1999

+ In *Buckley v. American Constitutional Law Foundation,* the U.S. Supreme Court invalidates a Colorado law that requires petition circulators to wear identification badges and meet strict reporting requirements.
+ A meeting of the World Trade Organizations (WTO) in Seattle, Washington, prompts massive antiglobalization demonstrations, ushering in a new era of protests.

2000

+ Large demonstrations are held at the Republican National Convention in Philadelphia and at the Democratic National Convention in Los Angeles.
+ In *Boy Scouts of America v. Dale,* the U.S. Supreme Court holds that the right of the Boy Scouts to expel a gay scout leader is guaranteed by freedom of association.

2001

+ In the wake of the September 11 attacks, Congress passes the USA PATRIOT Act, increasing the powers of the government and raising serious concerns among civil libertarians.

2003

+ Massive demonstrations are held throughout the United States (and across the world) protesting the plans of President George W. Bush to invade Iraq.

2004

+ 250,000 people march in New York City to protest the Republican National Convention.

2005

+ The inauguration of President George W. Bush on January 20 prompts numerous "counter-inaugural" protests in Washington, D.C., London, and Tokyo.

Appendix

Excerpts from Documents Relating to Assembly, Association, and Petition

The Bill of Rights, First Amendment, 1791

The U.S. Constitution did not contain a declaration of personal rights. This omission was remedied by the adoption of the Bill of Rights by the First Congress in 1789, which was ratified in 1791. The Bill of Rights contains 10 amendments.

Congress shall make no law respecting an establishment of religion, or prohibiting the free exercise thereof; or abridging the freedom of speech, or of the press, or the right of the people peaceably to assemble, and to petition the Government for a redress of grievances.

State Constitutions

Two states, Minnesota and New Mexico, do not provide for freedom of assembly and the right to petition in their constitutions. The other 48 guarantee these rights in various ways. Even before the Bill of Rights was added to the U.S. Constitution in 1791, guaranteeing individual rights including the freedom of assembly, many state constitutions had already been adopted promising just that.

ALABAMA CONSTITUTION, 1819
Article I
Section 25 Right to peaceably assemble and petition for redress of grievances, etc.
That the citizens have a right, in a peaceable manner, to assemble together for the common good, and to apply to those invested with the power of government for redress of grievances or other purposes, by petition, address, or remonstrance.

ALASKA CONSTITUTION, 1959
Article I
Section 6 Assembly; Petition
The right of the people peaceable to assemble, and to petition the government shall never be abridged.

ARIZONA CONSTITUTION, 1910
Article II
Section 5 Right of petition and of assembly.
The right of petition, and of the people peaceably to assemble for the common good, shall never be abridged.

ARKANSAS CONSTITUTION, 1874
Article II
Section 4 Right of the assembly and petition.
The right of the people to assemble to consult for the common good, and to petition, by address or remonstrance, the government, or any department thereof, shall never be abridged.

CALIFORNIA CONSTITUTION, 1849
Article I
Section 3
The people have the right to instruct their representatives, petition government for redress of grievances, and assemble freely to consult for the common good.

COLORADO CONSTITUTION, 1876
Article II
Section 24 Right to assemble and petition.
The people have the right peaceably to assemble for the common good, and to apply to those invested with the powers of government for redress of grievances, by petition or remonstrance.

CONNECTICUT CONSTITUTION, 1965
Article First
Section 14
The citizens have a right, in a peaceable manner, to assemble for their common good, and to apply to those invested with the powers of government, for redress of grievances, or other proper purposes, by petition, address or remonstrance.

DELAWARE CONSTITUTION, 1897
Article I
Section 16 Right of assembly; petition for redress of grievances.
Although disobedience to laws by a part of the people, upon suggestions of impolicy or injustice in them, tends by immediate effect and the influence of example not only to endanger the public welfare and safety, but also in governments of a republican form contravenes the social principles of such governments, founded on common consent for common good; yet the citizens have a right in an orderly manner to meet together, and to apply to persons entrusted with the powers of government, for redress of grievances or other proper purposes, by petition, remonstrance or address.

FLORIDA CONSTITUTION, 1885
Article I
Section 5 Right to assemble.
The people shall have the right peaceably to assemble, to instruct their representatives, and to petition for redress of grievances.

GEORGIA CONSTITUTION, 1777
Article I
Paragraph 9 Right to assemble and petition.
The people have the right to assemble peaceably for their common good and to apply by petition or remonstrance to those vested with the powers of government for redress of grievances.

HAWAII CONSTITUTION, 1978
Article I
Section 4 Freedom of religion, speech, press, assembly and petition.
No law shall be enacted respecting an establishment of religion, or prohibiting the free exercise thereof, or abridging the freedom of speech or of the press or the right of the people peaceably to assemble and to petition the government for a redress or grievances.

IDAHO CONSTITUTION, 1890
Article I
Section 10 Right of assembly.
The people shall have the right to assemble in a peaceable manner, to consult for their common good; to instruct their representatives, and to petition the legislature for the redress of grievances.

ILLINOIS CONSTITUTION, 1970
Article I
Section 5 Right to assemble and petition.
The people have the right to assemble in a peaceable manner, to consult for the common good, to make known their opinions to their representatives and to apply for redress of grievances.

INDIANA CONSTITUTION, 1851
Article I
Section 31 Right of assemblage and petition.
No law shall restrain any of the inhabitants of the State from assembling together in a peaceable manner, to consult for their common good; nor from instructing their representatives; nor from applying to the General Assembly for redress of grievances.

IOWA CONSTITUTION, 1857
Article I
Section 20 Right of assemblage—petition.
The people have the right freely to assemble together to counsel for the common good; to make known their opinions to their representatives and to petition for a redress of grievances.

KANSAS CONSTITUTION, 1862
Bill of Rights
Section 3 Right of peaceable assembly; petition.
The people have the right to assemble, in a peaceable manner, to consult for their common good, to instruct their representatives, and to petition the government, or any department thereof, for the redress of grievances.

KENTUCKY CONSTITUTION, 1792
Article I
Section 1
The right of assembling together in a peaceable manner for their common good, and of applying to those invested with the power of government for redress of grievances or other proper purposes, by petition, address or remonstrance.

LOUISIANA CONSTITUTION, 1974
Article I
Section 9 Right of Assembly and Petition.
No law shall impair the right of any person to assemble peaceably or to petition government for a redress of grievances.

MAINE CONSTITUTION, 1820
Article I
Section 15 Right of petition.
The people have a right at all times in an orderly and peaceable manner to assemble to consult upon the common good, to give instructions to their representatives, and to request, of either department of the government by petition or remonstrance, redress of their wrongs and grievances.

MARYLAND CONSTITUTION, 1867
Article I
Article 12
That for redress of grievances, and for amending, strengthening and preserving the Laws, the Legislature ought to be frequently convened.

Article 13
That every man hath a right to petition the Legislature for the redress of grievances in a peaceable and orderly manner.

MASSACHUSETTS CONSTITUTION, 1780
Part the First
Article XIX
The people have a right, in an orderly and peaceable manner, to assemble to consult upon the common good; give instructions to their representatives, and to request of the legislative body, by the way of addresses, petitions, or remonstrances, redress of the wrongs done them, and of the grievances they suffer.

MICHIGAN CONSTITUTION, 1963
Article I
Section 3 Assembly, consultation, instruction, petition.
The people have the right peaceably to assemble, to consult for common good, to instruct their representatives and to petition the government for redress of grievances.

MISSISSIPPI CONSTITUTION, 1890
Article 3
Section 11
The right of the people peaceably to assemble and petition the government on any subject shall never be impaired.

MISSOURI CONSTITUTION, 1875
Article I
Section 9 Rights of peaceable assembly and petition.
That the people have the right peaceably to assemble for their common good, and to apply to those invested with the powers of government for redress of grievances by petition or remonstrance.

MONTANA CONSTITUTION, 1889
Article II
Section 6 Freedom of assembly.
The people shall have the right peaceably to assemble, petition for redress or peaceably protest governmental action.

NEBRASKA CONSTITUTION, 1875
Article I
Section 19 Right of peaceable assembly and to petition government.
The right of the people peaceably to assemble to consult for the common good, and to petition the government, or any department thereof, shall never be abridged.

NEVADA CONSTITUTION, 1864
Article I
Section 10 Right to assemble and to petition.
The people shall have the right freely to assemble together to consult for the common good, to instruct their representatives and to petition the Legislature for redress of grievances.

NEW HAMPSHIRE CONSTITUTION, 1783
Part First
Article 32 Rights of Assembly, Instruction, and Petition.
The people have a right, in an orderly and peaceable manner, to assemble and consult upon the common good, give instructions to their representatives, and to request of the legislative body, by way of petition or remonstrance, redress of the wrongs done them, and of the grievances they suffer.

NEW JERSEY CONSTITUTION, 1947
Article I
Section 18
The people have the right freely to assemble together, to consult for the common good, to make known their opinions to their representatives, and to petition for redress of grievances.

NEW YORK CONSTITUTION, 1938
Article I
Section 9.1
No law shall be passed abridging the rights of the people peaceably to assemble and to petition the government.

NORTH CAROLINA CONSTITUTION, 1776
Article I
Section 12 Right of assembly and petition.
The people have a right to assemble together to consult for their common good, to instruct their representatives, and to apply to the General Assembly for redress of grievances; but secret political societies are dangerous to the liberties of a free people and shall not be tolerated.

NORTH DAKOTA CONSTITUTION, 2000
Article I
Section 5
The citizens have a right, in a peaceable manner, to assemble together for the common good, and to apply to those invested with the powers of government for the redress of grievances, or for other proper purposes, by petition, address or remonstrance.

OHIO CONSTITUTION, 1851
Article I
Section 1.03 Right to assemble.
The people have the right to assemble together, in a peaceable manner, to consult for their common good; to instruct their representatives; and to petition the general assembly for the redress of grievances.

OKLAHOMA CONSTITUTION, 1907
Article II
Section II-3 Right of assembly and petition.
The people have the right peaceably to assemble for their own good, and to apply to those invested with the powers of government for redress of grievances by petition, address, or remonstrance.

OREGON CONSTITUTION, 1859
Article I
Section 26 Assemblages of people; instruction of representatives; application to legislature.
No law shall be passed restraining any of the inhabitants of the State from assembling together in a peaceable manner to consult for their

common good; nor from instructing their Representatives; nor from applying to the Legislature for redress of greviances [sic].

PENNSYLVANIA CONSTITUTION, 1776
Article I
Section 20
The citizens have a right in a peaceable manner to assemble together for their common good, and to apply to those invested with the powers of government for redress of grievances or other proper purposes, by petition, address or remonstrance.

RHODE ISLAND CONSTITUTION, 1843
Article I
Section 21 Right to assembly—Redress of grievances—Freedom of speech.
The citizens have a right in a peaceable manner to assembly for their common good, and to apply to those invested with the powers of government, for redress of grievances, or for other purposes, by petition, address, or remonstrance.

SOUTH CAROLINA CONSTITUTION, 1778
Article I
Section 2 Religious freedom; freedom of speech; right of assembly and petition.
The General Assembly shall make no law respecting an establishment of religion or prohibiting the free exercise thereof, or abridging the freedom of speech or of the press; or the right of the people peaceably to assemble and to petition the government or any department thereof for a redress of grievances.

SOUTH DAKOTA CONSTITUTION, 1889
Article VI
Section 4. Right of petition and peaceable assembly.
The right of petition, and of the people peaceably to assemble to consult for the common good and make known their opinions, shall never be abridged.

TENNESSEE CONSTITUTION, 1796
Article I
Section 23. Right of assembly.
That the citizens have a right, in a peaceable manner, to assemble together for their common good, to instruct their representatives, and

to apply to those invested with the powers of government for redress of grievances, or other proper purposes, by address or remonstrance.

TEXAS CONSTITUTION, 1876

Article I

Section 27. Right of assembly; petition for redress of grievances.

The citizens shall have the right, in a peaceable manner, to assemble together for their common good; and apply to those invested with the powers of government for redress of grievances or other purposes, by petition, address or remonstrance.

UTAH CONSTITUTION, 1894

Article I

Section 1 Inherent and inalienable rights.

All men have the inherent and inalienable right to enjoy and defend their lives and liberties; to acquire, possess and protect property; to worship according to the dictates of their consciences; to assemble peaceably, protest against wrongs, and petition for redress of grievances; to communicate freely their thoughts and opinions, being responsible for the abuse of that right.

VERMONT CONSTITUTION, 1777

Chapter I

Article 20. Right to assemble, instruct and petition.

That the people have a right to assemble together to consult for their common good—to instruct their Representatives—and to apply to the Legislature for redress of grievances, by address, petition or remonstrance.

VIRGINIA CONSTITUTION, 1776

Article I

Section 12 Freedom of speech and of the press; right peaceably to assemble, and to petition.

That the freedoms of speech and of the press are among the great bulwarks of liberty, and can never be restrained except by despotic governments; that any citizen may freely speak, write, and publish his sentiments on all subjects, being responsible for the abuse of that right; that the General Assembly shall not pass any law abridging the freedom of speech or of the press, nor the right of the people peaceably to assemble, and to petition the government for the redress of grievances.

WASHINGTON CONSTITUTION, 1889
Article I
Section 4. Right of petition and assemblage.
The right of petition and of the people peaceably to assemble for the common good shall never be abridged.

WEST VIRGINIA CONSTITUTION, 1872
Article III
Section 16 Right of public assembly held inviolate.
The right of the people to assemble in a peaceable manner, to consult for the common good, to instruct their representatives, or to apply for redress of grievances, shall be held inviolate.

WISCONSIN CONSTITUTION, 1848
Article I
Section 4 Right to assemble and petition.
The right of the people peaceably to assemble, to consult for the common good, and to petition the government, or any department thereof, shall never be abridged.

WYOMING CONSTITUTION, 1889
Article I
Section 21 Right of petition and peaceable assembly.
The right of petition, and of the people peaceably to assemble to consult for the common good, and to make known their opinions, shall never be denied or abridged.

Further Reading

Books

Atkinson, Linda. *Mother Jones: The Most Dangerous Woman in America.* New York: Crown, 1978.

Bernard, Catherine. *Sojourner Truth: Abolitionist and Women's Rights Activist.* Berkeley Heights, N.J.: Enslow, 2001.

Bober, Natalie S. *Abigail Adams: Witness to a Revolution.* New York: Simon & Schuster/Atheneum, 1995.

Colman, Penny. *Fannie Lou Hamer and the Right to Vote.* Brookfield, Conn.: Millbrook Press, 1993.

Cuomo, Kerry Kennedy. *Speak Truth to Power: Human Rights Defenders Who Are Changing Our World.* New York: Crown Publishers, 2000.

Dash, Joan. *We Shall Not Be Moved: The Women's Factory Strike of 1909.* New York: Scholastic, 1996.

Doyle, William. *An American Insurrection: The Battle of Oxford, Mississippi, 1962.* New York: Doubleday, 2001.

Friese, Kai. *Rosa Parks: The Movement Organizes.* Englewood Cliffs, N.J.: Silver Burdett Press, 1990.

Fritz, Jean. *You Want Women to Vote, Lizzie Stanton?* New York: Putnam, 1995.

Issacs, Sally S. *America in the Time of Susan B. Anthony.* Des Plaines, Ill.: Heinemann, 2000.

Johnston, Norma. *Remember the Ladies: The First Women's Rights Convention.* New York: Scholastic, 1995.

Rappaport, Doreen. *The Boston Coffee Party.* Illus. by Emily Arnold McCully. New York: Harper & Row, 1988.

Von Drehle, David. *Triangle: The Fire that Changed America.* New York: Atlantic Monthly Press, 2003.

Bibliography

Bartley, Numan V. *The Rise of Massive Resistance: Race and Politics in the South During the 1950s.* Baton Rouge: Louisiana State University Press, 1969.

Branch, Taylor. *Parting the Waters: America in the King Years 1954–63.* New York: Simon & Schuster, 1988.

Burns, Stewart, ed. *Daybreak of Freedom: The Montgomery Bus Boycott.* Chapel Hill: University of North Carolina Press, 1997.

Chang, Nancy. *Silence Political Dissent: How Post-September 11 Anti-Terrorism Measures Threaten Our Civil Liberties.* New York: Seven Stories Press, 2002.

Garey, Diane. *Defending Everybody: A History of the American Civil Liberties Union.* New York: TV Books, 1998.

Gitlin, Todd. *The Sixties: Years of Hope, Days of Rage.* New York: Bantam, 1987.

Hamlin, David. *The Nazi/Skokie Conflict.* Boston: Beacon Press, 1980.

Irons, Peter. *Justice at War.* New York: Oxford University Press, 1983.

Klurman, Michael J. *From Jim Crow to Civil Rights: The Supreme Court and the Struggle for Racial Equality.* New York: Oxford University Press, 2004.

Kraditor, Aileen. *The Ideas of the Woman Suffrage Movement, 1890–1920.* New York: Columbia University Press, 1965.

Loery, Robert D., ed. *The Civil Rights Act of 1964: The Passage of the Law That Ended Racial Segregation.* Albany: State University of New York Press, 1997.

McGerr, Michael. *A Fierce Discontent: The Rise and Fall of the Progressive Movement in America 1870–1920.* New York: Free Press, 2003.

Schrecker, Ellen. *Many Are the Crimes: McCarthyism in America.* Boston: Little, Brown, 1998.

Smith, Marc A., and Kollock, Peter, eds. *Communities in Cyberspace.* London: Routledge, 1999.

Walker, Samuel. *In Defense of American Liberties: A History of the ACLU, Second Edition.* Carbondale: Southern Illinois University Press, 1990, 1999.

Zinn, Howard. *A People's History of the United States: 1492 to Present.* New York: HarperCollins, 1999.

Web Sites

Baird, Charles W. "On the Right to Strike," Liberty Haven. Available online. URL: http://www.libertyhaven.com/politicsandcurrent events/unionsandotherorganizations/righttostrike.html. Downloaded on October 12, 2004.

Bexte, Martina. "The Vietnam War Protests," PageWise. Available online. URL: http://ohoh.essortment.com/vietnamwarprot_rlcz.htm. Downloaded on October 12, 2004.

Georgakas, Dan. "Hollywood Blacklist," Encyclopedia of the American Left. Available online. URL: http://www.writing.upenn.edu/~afilreis/50s/blacklist.html. Downloaded on October 12, 2004.

Hudson, David L., Jr. "Civil Rights & First Amendment," First Amendment Center. Available online. URL: http://www.firstamendment-center.org/assembly/topic.aspx?topic=civil_rights. Downloaded on October 12, 2004.

————. "Freedom of Assembly," First Amendment Center. Available online. URL: http://www.firstamendmentcenter.org/assembly/overview.aspx. Downloaded on October 12, 2004.

Reese, Michael. "The Cold War and Red Scare in Washington State," The Center for the Study of the Pacific Northwest. Available online. URL: http://www.washington.edu/uwired/outreach/cspn/curcan/main.html. Downloaded on October 12, 2004.

"Rights of Individuals: Civil and Political," Human and Constitutional Rights, Arthur W. Diamond Library, Columbia Law School. Available online. URL: http://www.hrcr.org/chart/civil+political/freedoms.html. Downloaded on October 12, 2004.

Stricker, Heather. "Assembly on Private Property," First Amendment Center. Available online. URL: http://www.firstamendmentcenter.org/assembly/topic.aspx?topic=private property. Downloaded on October 12, 2004.

Index

Page numbers in *italic* indicate photographs. Page numbers in **boldface** indicate box features and margin quotations. Page numbers followed by *m* indicate maps. Page numbers followed by *t* indicate tables or graphs. Page numbers followed by *g* indicate glossary entries. Page numbers followed by *c* indicate chronology entries.